PORTRAIT

40 YEARS IN PORN

David Christopher
with Matthew Klane

Cover and Interior Design by
Vinnie Corbo and Matthew Klane

Published by Volossal Publishing
www.volossal.com

CONTENTS

Introduction   5

I

Chapter 1: The Golden Age   9
Chapter 2 : Sharon   23
Chapter 3: Volunteer of America   39
Chapter 4: Some Like it Hot   53
Chapter 5: Social Studies   67

II

Chapter 6: More, More, More   81
Chapter 7: Candice   95
Chapter 8: Coast to Coast   107
Chapter 9: Big Top   123
Chapter 10: Bone Voyage   137

III

Chapter 11: Goldie and JJ   151
Chapter 12: The Pipe Bomb   163
Chapter 13: Governor Pussyman   175
Chapter 14: Legend   189
Chapter 15: It's My Party   201

The Credits   215

My name is Bernie Cohen a.k.a. David Christopher. Pussyman. I live in Encino, California. Best fucking dog park in the whole country! I've lived in Marina del Rey and Santa Monica. You'd figure Santa Monica would have tremendous dog parks. Rich, liberal, da da da. Terrible. *Horrible!* Gravel up a hill. Here, in Encino, there are miles and miles of different kinds of fields. Athletic fields. Walking fields. Ponds. Kayaking. Dog parks! So that's why I'm in Encino. I love dogs.

Before I moved here, I lived in Tarzana, the next town over. It was named for – what's his name? – Edgar Rice Burroughs. The guy who wrote *Tarzan.* You should have seen my other house! It was so fucking unique. Unlike any other house in the Valley. I had this huge cabin, you know, like the ones in Lake Tahoe, with gorgeous land and beautiful trees. There was actually a tree growing *inside the house,* right in the middle, up through the roof. And there were these eclectic homes throughout the neighborhood. Not one house was the same. There was a giant house, next to a modern house, next to some small little nothing. Like anyone, someone making $10,000 a year, could have been living there. That area is tremendous, and I lived there for seven years from 2001-2008. But when the industry went kaput, I needed a smaller house and moved here.

My friend Glenn was living across the street. I walked into this place and saw the tall ceilings. I thought, "Wow! This is perfect." It sort of reminded me of a loft from my days in New York City. Lots of light. Good for shooting. Because the best places to shoot are these little homes. This way, no one knows what you're doing. And you definitely don't want anyone to know. That's the last thing you want! Plus, there was a nice backyard for my dogs. And it was right up the street from the dog park. So here I am.

I

CHAPTER 1
THE GOLDEN AGE

They call the '70s "The Golden Age of Porn." I don't think so. For me, "The Golden Age" was the '90s. There's a big difference. The '70s were great for acting because everyone wanted to become a legitimate actor. They thought, "Wow! What a great way to break into show business." Go to real acting school and then work on these two-three week movies. These were big movies with big scripts, you know, tons and tons of dialogue, and these people could act *somewhat*. But the filmmaking was not good. The cameramen didn't know how to shoot sex. They got all the wrong angles. Seriously. They didn't know anything!

And then there were people like me who didn't care about acting at all. What do I care about acting? I don't give a shit about acting. I wanted to be a teacher. I wanted to be a director. Those were the two things I cared about. Teaching and directing. I wanted to communicate what was happening at that particular time. The liberation of sexuality. I also wanted to explain myself, who I was and what I was doing, why I was making X-rated pictures. Because the model that most people have is that you are an asshole and a jerk if you do stuff like this. They say, "You're in porno? You must be a nasty person." It's completely wrong. I've met tons of wonderful *intelligent* people in this business. Everyone thinks, "Oh, she's stupid." Why? Because she's taking her clothes off? That doesn't make her stupid. She's expressing her sexuality. She likes to show herself off. What's the big deal? It's good. Power! Power of the woman!

That's what I would always say. I used to have fights with real "Feminazis" – as my friend Mike Graffone calls them –

who fall back to their fundamentalist way of thinking. Even though they want freedom of sexuality, they still think, in porno, the women are getting abused by men. That men are forcing them to do it. I mean, directors will make actors and actresses do things. Because they're directors. They direct! But that whole other idea is bullshit. On the other hand, I can't stand chauvinists. Like at the dog park here, when people found out how I was this '90s big shot who had directed, produced, and starred in X-rated movies, they absolutely loved me! Certain guys, mostly blue-collar guys, they thought I was like an unbelievable hero. They'd ask me all of the typical male chauvinistic kinds of questions. And after I gave them my raps, you know, they would look at me like, "What the fuck are you talking about?"

I promote the power of female sexuality. There are probably some directors doing that now, but for years, no one did. That's why Pussyman was so different. I didn't care if the guy had an orgasm. In X-rated movies, you know, the scenes end with a male orgasm. The quote unquote "pop shot." To prove to the audience that the sex was real. That's how it started. Proof is in the pudding! Over the years, it's gotten to the point where if you don't cum at the end of a scene, then you won't be working much longer. I never really believed in that, but because of the nature of the business, in my movies, I've had to follow suit. And I've made *a lot* of movies!

*

I started in porn to help pay for grad school. That was 1975. So, you know, half of the '70s, the '80s, the '90s, and since. What's that, four decades? I've been in and out of porn for 40 years. Wow! Not many people have been in the business all this time. One other guy: Joey Silvera. There might still be a few people sitting behind a desk, but no one is working on the sets. Just me and Joey Silvera.

I had other jobs in the meantime. I taught high school for a while. And I managed this huge record store in New

York City called Disc-o-Mat. On 34th street near Penn Station. And then I went back to work for my dad. He called me up and said, "It's an emergency." So I came home to Boston and would drive back to New York on the weekends. I was married then, to Lisa, my first wife. That's when her father offered me the territories of Long Island, Westchester, parts of New Jersey, parts of Connecticut. He sold lighting fixtures, you know, chandeliers. He told me that he was retiring soon and his business was worth a couple hundred grand a year. So I put on my sport jacket and went around the suburbs. After like four months, he said to me: "I want you to try and break into Manhattan." Okay. Here I am, doing this job, you know, bored as shit, but there could have been a lot of money in it for me.

One day, in Manhattan, I passed a place called Show World. The biggest sex emporium in New York City. Famous for years. It had five floors. On one floor, there was a regular strip theater. On another, there were girls in booths. All different things. So I'm walking past, and my friend popped out. He said, "I'm the manager here. You want to work? I got some girl, and you can have sex with her." *He was really begging me!* I did it one time and hated it! Well, I did do some live shows later, you know, private things, 50 people on a Saturday night. But a live show in front of an audience of strangers that had just been walking around on the street? I said, "Listen, Joe." Oh yeah! It was Joey Silvera. He was the guy! I said, "Joe, I can't do this." The whole thing was just stupid. They're staring at you. Some are probably jerking off in the corner. Who knows? Those theaters are dark, you know what I mean? And you're up on fucking stage.

So I continued selling chandeliers. Of course, a few months later, my father-in-law came to me and said – can you guess? – he said, "I'm sorry, Bernie. I'm not retiring! I'm not giving up so quick! I have a couple more years left in me." That's about when I said, "Fuck this!" and began making movies full-time. But now I'm kind of ahead of myself! Should I tell the story of how I first got into porno? Quickly.

It's a great story. How I did one scene and went on from there. Because I was really just doing a lot of commercials. As a PA, you know, Production Assistant. I got the job from my friend Michael, my roommate in college, who wanted to be in the film business. There was this pocketbook called *The New York Guide to Something or Other.* He went around to every little company in the book until he found a job as a PA. One day, he asked me: "Do you want some extra work? You could be a PA, too."

The first movies that I worked on were commercials. I remember a few with Joe Namath for some shaving product. Schick, maybe? They would bring in a crew and make a film. Director. Cameraman. Lighting man. The whole bit. And, in those days, people that made commercials also made porno movies. Same exact companies. They made commercials. They made industrial films. They made porno movies. Many times, someone might be great at shooting a commercial, so they'd hire the guy for an X-rated picture. It was horrible! He would get so flustered by seeing naked people that he couldn't shoot straight. He was out of focus. He was over here somewhere when he should have been over there. And they didn't really concentrate on sexuality, you know, they would just shoot it like a regular film. They didn't care about angles. It's all about the angles! But no one knew that then. No one even brought it up! No one.

And that's how it went. For years.

*

I've always wanted to do a book and tell every aspect of the business from my perspective. Why I went into it, what actually takes place on the sets, the lifestyle, the different people, through the decades. Acting, writing, directing, running companies. Because I've done it all. And I've always wanted to, well, communicate. I'm a communicator.

Seven years ago, the year before Obama, I was set up with a writer. He had done biographies with some famous sports people. Joe Namath? Could have been Joe Namath. Or Nolan Ryan? That name sticks out for some reason. We had four or five meetings, and then he went to Vermont. Just for a trip. He was married, but he met some girl on a hippie commune farm up there. Yeah, he met some girl with two kids and fell in love. He sent a – what do you call it? – Dear John. But for a female. What do you a call a female Dear John letter? Dear Whatever. Dear Mary. I don't know. I only know Dear John. Dear John is "you've been dumped." A guy has been dumped by a girl. But the opposite? I don't know what the opposite is. Anyway, he dumped his fucking wife here and married the girl with the two kids and became a hippie commune guy in Vermont. I didn't realize they still had those places. Vermont's a great state!

And that was the end of the bookmaking for a while. I did try to write it myself, but that was terrible! I just can't focus. I probably have – what's that called when you can't focus? – A.D.D. Yep. I definitely have slight A.D.D. I had a friend with *heavy* A.D.D., and she gave me these pills, but I hated them. It was horrid! I was up all night. They made me like speedy, you know what I mean? At times, though, I definitely have a little A.D.D. Focusing just ends. You could be telling me anything, and I won't hear it. Any time you talk about machines that happens to me! My whole life, I've had this battle with machines. It's bad, man. Many people have tried to teach me computers. I even paid this guy, you know, to come to my house and give me lessons. Everything he said just went right over my head. It was like a wicked science!

Science was always my worst subject. I was good in English and History. And sports! And pop culture! I had so many records. "Hit the Road Jack" was my first 45. And my father gave me "Mack the Knife" by Bobby Darin. That was 1960 when I was ten years old. "Roses Are Red (My Love)" by Bobby Vinton was the first 45 that I actually went out and bought myself. "It's My Party": Leslie Gore. "Locomation": Little Eva. The Four Seasons first record: "Sherry." I remember them all. Like I just saw

Clint Eastwood's movie about the Four Seasons called *Jersey Boys*, and they were singing these old songs from the '60s. I knew every single one of them – boom! – I could name their first seven hits. And yet, I can't remember my favorite movie director from, you know, last week. But I remember every single record and when they came out *in order*. I can remember that perfectly! So I still remember things. Don't worry about that!

I just can't remember... Christopher Nolan. He's my favorite director! I loved *Inception*. I thought *Inception* was spectacular. I watched it seven times. And I loved the way he did *Batman*. His original picture was called *Memento*. Tremendous. I watched the whole movie – this is like a year ago – and when it ended, I went to bed immediately. I don't know. I must have been tired. Anyway, I woke up the next morning and – guess what? – I couldn't remember the entire ending. I had no idea what happened! The picture *Memento* is about a guy who forgets constantly. Like he'll see you, and ten seconds later, he'll forget who you are. So he illustrated his whole body with pictures of things that were important to him. And he took little snapshots of everything. He had like a 1,000 snapshots. And he would write on them where and when he saw this person or that person or whatever. So he'd write and take his little Polaroids and he was like an illustrated man.

As opposed to now, these porno girls are all like illustrated women. They're all tatted up from the bottom to the top. Across their tits. Everywhere! More and more and more. I just shot a movie and like four out of the five girls were entirely illustrated. I see more girls with tats now than guys! Because, originally, who got tats? Military men. They got shipped to some foreign post and put their mothers or their girlfriends on their arms. I remember, in like 1990, there was only one actress who had tats. And hardly anyone would hire her. She was basically blackballed. No one wanted to see tats back in 1990. This tat thing started like five years ago and has just gotten bigger and bigger. Every new girl that comes into the business now is covered in tats. Like tons of them! Amazing! Why am I talking about tats?

*

I think my father might have had a little tattoo. I can't remember. If he did, then it wasn't a very good one. Because they didn't really make good tattoos in those days. They would just throw a little something on for the army guys. My father was in the army, but he was on the planes. You didn't have to be in the Air Force to get put on a plane. And if you were a Jew, then they would make you a shooter, right in the open part. Oh yeah. I found that out from different places. Here and there. Jews go to the open part of the plane, you know what I mean? Of course! They'll be the first ones to get shot! But they'll also be doing the shooting.

During the war, no one really knew much about the camps or anything that was going on. But afterwards, my father was obsessed. When he wasn't working, or working out, he would sit in front of the television. He'd either watch the Sox game or anything that had to do with the Nazis. He spent hours and hours watching shows about the Holocaust. To the point where, me and my sister, we would make jokes about it, you know, I kind of understand. There's this tremendous new station on television called American Hero. They do the greatest job ever of covering WWI and WWII. From these shows, I've learned so much that I didn't know before. And I knew a lot. I love history! So I can watch these Hitler shows for hours. I'll be watching a game and then switch over, you know, on the commercial. What's going on here? Some great battle. Some great general I didn't know before. This and that. Dwight Eisenhower smoking cigarettes, one after another, after another.

When I was younger though, what did I care? I'm basically anti-war. Vietnam was just beginning. I don't want to hear about your fucking wars. "Okay, dad. I know what you did." I mean, at least I know what he told me. My mother – the Mars!

– who knows what she did? She used to always tell me, she'd say, "Bernie, it's alright to have little white lies. Just don't do anything really bad." Don't rob. Don't murder. Don't fuck with people, you know what I mean? But little white lies are okay... and she had *huge* white lies! First of all, she had been married before. To a doctor. From New York! Who wasn't even Jewish! And her mother, my grandmother, pleaded with her to come back to Boston and find herself a nice Jew. Even though this guy she married was a doctor! So eventually, after a couple of years, she came home.

I think that's when, somehow, her age magically changed and – boom! – she was ten years younger. She had already been married and didn't want anyone to know. My mother did not want to be an old maid. And here she was, again, in her 30s now, looking for a guy, and needing to be set up. I think they were introduced. I'm pretty sure that's how it happened. Abraham and Frances Cohen. And the whole time, my father was like five years younger than my mother. But he always thought he was five years older! Yeah, my aunt Rosamond told me that. I haven't spoken to her in years. I don't even know if she's still alive. But when I went back to Boston for my mother's funeral, she said to me: "You know, your mother was the oldest one in the whole family. Look at her birth certificate. You'll see how old she really is."

I thought she was 81. And she was 91! The Mars was ten years older than we thought! And previously married! That's two "little white lies." They didn't hurt anyone, though, right? So what's the difference?

*

Today is the 1ˢᵗ of June. When I woke up this morning, it was cloudy and freezing. I didn't know how many jackets to wear. An hour later, at the dog park, the sun is shining. That's the way it'll be all month here in Los Angeles. "June Gloom." That's what they call it. And I'll be 65 years old this month. I was born in 1950, right in the middle of the century.

I don't really remember anything big from the '50s. White picket fences. Everyone wore the same clothes. The men wore suits. Unless they were blue-collar workers and then they wore uniforms. Women all wore the same outfits. Everyone was the same! But the economy was doing great. The soldiers came back from the war and received money from the government to buy a house. Start a little family. That's how people got their original homes. My parents probably paid like $3,000 for the place in Sharon Heights. South Main Street. A few miles from where the Patriots now play in Foxborough. I still remember details from that house. Like when I was seven years old, and my cousin – who now lives in Beverly Hills – would come over. He would take the train to Sharon and stay over at our place for the weekend. I remember playing croquet or volleyball in the backyard. Badminton.

When I was 12 years old, my father set up these bags in the basement. Small bags. Heavy bags. He wanted to teach me how to be a boxer. He was in a lot of amateur fights and wanted me to follow in his footsteps. He was a puncher, you know, lefty, 5'6", kind of small, but a *tough guy*. Big shoulders. Back then, all of the men wore those little white T-shirts. The "guinea Tee" – what do call them? – wife-beaters. And that's what he always wore. Or do you remember those original male bathing suits like the big fat wrestlers used to wear. The one-piece things with the little strap. I've seen pictures of my father as a young man, and he was wearing one of those. Striking some pose. Listen, if you run your own business – a meat market no less! – and you have to deal with the Mob and the government both, then you better be a tough motherfucker! That's for sure.

So it's kind of funny, you know, I boxed a lot when I was young. I went to a couple of camps, and there was always boxing. Around the neighborhood, we'd always set up boxing matches. I had the headgear and everything. I didn't really like boxing, but I was quick. Good with the jab. Until, one day, I fought this guy who was like 20 lbs. heavier than me. A southpaw like my father. He hit me with a left hook, and –

boom! – I saw stars and went down. I didn't get up. After that, I said, "Dad, I quit. I retire. That's the end." I wasn't cut out to be a boxer. Just like I wasn't cut out to be a meat man!

*

State Beef. That's what it was called. When I was a kid, it was a small company of only four or five people. My father, my uncle Danny, a couple of other guys. I remember him bringing me down to Faneuil Hall Marketplace. That's where he was for years. Until my freshman year in high school when they built a big packing plant. As far as I'm concerned, that plant was one of the worst places I've ever been in my entire life! Giant slabs of beef. The trucks would come roaring in at like 4:00 in the morning. These guys would be all speeded up. Black Beauties. They drove in from the Midwest, you know, Iowa or Nebraska, all night, nonstop. It's freezing outside, and inside, it's even colder! And the workers would pull those slabs off the truck and hang them up, you know, just like in *Rocky*.

The environment inside was totally disgusting. All that hanging beef made its way to these cutting tables. The meat cutters, they'd slam the thing down, and each would carve his section. Like an assembly line. Everyone's drilling. Knifing. Blood is everywhere! Guys are just hacking and swearing at each other. And if they were mad at my father, or mad at their wives, they'd take some stuff off of the floor and toss it in with the hot dog meat. Grind it all together. That's why I don't eat hot dogs! After I saw how they were made, I said, "That's it. I'm done with hot dogs, man." I knew this wasn't the only place where this was happening, you know what I mean? There were graders and inspectors, but they wouldn't pay attention. The meat just got packaged up and sent out.

When I first started working there, he was doing big business with Friendly's. They were out in Springfield. But, eventually, he saw that there was more money to be made doing business with the government. My father was a supplier for the U.S. Army, the Air Force, the Navy. He sold them different cuts of meat. And tons and tons of ground hamburger. I remember working there in 1972, fresh out of college, the year Nixon ran against McGovern. And Massachusetts was the only state that voted for McGovern. Nixon! The biggest asshole ever and he won every state! At work, I had fights with everyone. Nixon had a group of blue-collar supporters called the Hardhats, and they were all over the meat market. I was always yelling, "Vote against the war! Vote for the Democrat!" In the end, my guy won, but he only won our state.

At this time, my father probably had 150 people working for him. He had expanded incredibly. That's when the unions came after him, and his business deteriorated. They became a unionized shop, you know, and immediately went on strike. They went on strike one year, and then the next year, they went on strike again. Somewhere in the middle, there was also a big scandal with the Mob. My father got into a battle with one of the union guy's brothers, or with the Mob, or something like that. I can't remember the exact deal, but my father was an honest man. He had *integrity*. He was one of the first to hire black people. No one hired black guys. My mother kept saying, "They'll cause you trouble in the end." The blacks. My mother said that. And I guess she was *a little* right. They were the ones that pushed for the union that led to the downfall of his place. Two strikes, two years in a row.

My mother worked, too. Always in banks. She was very good with numbers, my mother. And when it came to money, she was on the ball. Oh yeah. I remember her working at the Federal Reserve. I think she worked there for 25 years. Who knows what she did? I would drop her off at South Station and then go up the street to the meat market. Every summer, you know, when I would work for my father at that horrible fucking place. I was always thinking, "Man, I can't do this. No thank you! This is not going to be my life." You can understand that, can't you?

*

We were sort of the model '50s family: my father, my mother, me, and my sister Bonnie. I got along unbelievably with my sister. We were like *this*. She was my best friend. Bonnie was two years younger than me and followed everything I did. Like I was the captain of my neighborhood. I mean, everyone was really a bunch of nerds! So when it came to sports, I really stood out. I wasn't great, but *in my neighborhood*, I was tremendous. It was me who organized the basketball games. We had a big driveway, and there would be bicycle races. I'd always let Bonnie ride in those. And I also let her into the Olympics! We held our own Olympics, you know, and I'd let her be one of the countries. You weren't supposed to let little girls play with the boys in the Olympics. But I'd say, "She's not a little girl. She's my sister, and I bet she could beat half of you guys!" And she could.

I remember us dancing around the living room together. My parents would listen to show tunes. Or Frank Sinatra. Yeah, overall, I'd say that I had a very happy childhood. Spoiled is what I was! Things were done for me. Maybe that's why I can't do many things now. I speak to other people and they had to do *this*, clean *that*, da da da. My parents just said, "Go out there and have fun. Do good in school." And I got good grades, but not like Bonnie. She got all A's. I think she was the valedictorian. Right at the top! I was probably like 25th or something, but not first or second like my sister. Bonnie was definitely smarter than me. She was a genius! No doubt about it. And she could do so many other fucking things. She could fix anything. Meanwhile, no one else in my family could fix a thing. It was like she ran the whole house. And that's how she was to her friends, always there for everybody. She was just a great fucking person. There's nothing more that can be said. What a horrible shame.

You know, I'm the one who named her Bonnie! I don't know exactly when, but we were pretty young. Why did I start calling her that? Maybe I couldn't pronounce the name Roberta? Or maybe I was saying Bernie? Who knows? I just called her Bonnie, and then everyone picked it up. My theory, and she liked it too, is that we are given names by our parents that we have no control over. We might hate the name! If you're going through life for many, many years, and you're always called something, then you should be called something that you really like. It's you. You're the person! And even though I liked the name Bernard, eh, I really didn't. They would call me Ben*ahd*. And *Ber*nerd. I liked Andrew better. My middle name. That's a pretty classy name, I thought. So when David Christopher came to me, it was like, "Yeah! That's what I want to be called! That's who I am." That's who I *feel* like I am. It's much better than Bernard Cohen.

Only two people still call me Bernie. Joey Silvera. And my friend Michael, my roommate in college. That's it. To most everyone else, I'm David Christopher. Did I tell you how I got the name? I'll take care of that one right away. I was 25 years old and in grad school. I didn't have a porno name yet. I had used like five different names, but nothing that really stuck. I was living at the beach, you know, and here I was, driving, 6:00 at night, on my way to an evening class. You pull up along the beach and then cut across into the great part of Long Island. There was a beautiful sunset. Everything was beautiful! All of a sudden, I looked up, and it seemed like, coming down on my head, I can still kind of picture it: "DAVID." Messenger of the Jews. And then: "CHRIST-opher." But it wasn't Christopher. It was Christ. And the last part was -opher, o-p-h-e-r. David Christopher.

I thought, "Wow! What a great filmmaking name! A writer's name. A philosopher's name. That's who I am. That's who I'm supposed to be." And that's how I became David Christopher. Just like that. Just then.

CHAPTER 2
SHARON

One of my grad classes was on the history of female sexuality. I was the only guy in a room full of women and would constantly battle with my classmates. They're supposedly feminist, yet were still repressing anything to do with sex. Which is one of the ways that men have kept women down throughout history. Big time! Growing up, you could just feel the repression. It permeated everything. Women had to do a certain thing. Men had to do a certain thing. Even at 12 years old, I was thinking, "Wow! We're all wearing uniforms!" I didn't come to my exact theories on the evolvement of sexuality, you know, until college. I wrote this tremendous paper, 100 pages, I remember, all about the repression of sexuality over the centuries and how women were finally breaking out. I got it back, and my professor, she gave me a C. I was shocked! I thought that paper was an A+!

But even as a teenager, you know, I thought that women were being abused by men. Maybe I saw it with my parents? My father controlled everything, and my mother was totally submissive. She couldn't do anything! The Mars was the sweetest person in the world, but she couldn't cook. She couldn't clean. Those were the things that women were supposed to do. My father became the chef later because my mother was so horrible at cooking. "And such small portions!" You know the joke. That was her. One of the worst of all time! My mother made good chicken and that was it. I'm the only person I know who never even liked Peanut Butter & Jelly because of how she made it. And I hated tuna fish. She would put pickalilli in with tuna. Like this relish kind of thing. Ugh! She was just terrible at cooking. And cleaning. She never got deep into the cleaning. Surface level only. Oh yeah. She was great at that surface level. And… she was a sweetheart! That's the most important thing!

She was wonderful to talk to. Me and my mother, we could talk about anything, except she never really went into deep subjects like my father. He was always searching for the big answers, psychologically and philosophically. That's why he went back to school after he retired. He had always wanted to go to college, but never did because he had to go work in the meat market. He worked like a dog his whole life, you know what I mean? So when I was going to college, I think he was a little jealous. He would always try to have philosophy talks with me, you know, about different philosophers and theories that I was learning. Of course, he knew a couple of those Jewish guys who really pushed the Jewish philosophy. I can't remember their names, you know, Holocaust philosophers. *Man's Search for Meaning*. That kind of thing.

My father went to temple a lot. On Saturdays, of course, and Sundays for brunch. Lox and bagels. On the big holidays, he would get there at 8:00 in the morning and stay until 4:00 in the afternoon. He used to try and get me to go, but I'd stay there for an hour and leave. Put it this way: I never fasted. I tried a couple of times, you know, although by the afternoon, I'd be starving! And my mother, she told me: "It says in the Bible, if you feel like your body can't do it, then stop." She wasn't religious at all, my mother. Wasn't into it. Yeah, she'd go, and stand there with the other wives, but we didn't keep Kosher or anything. Are you kidding? Never. We didn't have like glasses for certain days. None of that! I was forced to go to Hebrew School, you know, to memorize the symbols. This and that. Da da da. And then I was Bar Mitzvah-ed and haven't gone back since.

My father was a Cohen, though, so I am, too. There are three Jewish tribes. The Cohens: the leaders. The Yisraels: the everyday people. And the Levis: I don't know who they are! That's why Cohen is one of the most popular Jewish names in America. It means you are a priest. So if you are a Jew and you have the name Cohen, then you're in luck, man. And most of the Cohens I've met, when I ask their history, they aren't real Cohens. They're like Yisraels whose ancestors changed their name when they arrived here. Regular people, you know, Rothenbergs or Greenbergs or something with -berg. And Sharon, where I grew up, it was *all Jews*. I think Sharon became a big place for Jews because the word "Sha*ron*" is somewhere in the Bible. It's like a big city or something. They came here and thought, "Sha*ron*. That's where Jews should live!" Like Canton. Lots of Chinese people live in Canton, don't they? I think they do.

*

Sharon was your typical deep suburban town buried halfway between Boston and Providence. And we had no influence from the cities. No one cared about Providence. We never went there. Boston would be the place that we cared about, but I didn't know what was going on in Boston. I didn't know anything about the world. Zero. Not a thing. Sharon, to me, was boring! That's why, as soon as I could, I left for New York City. To find out what was going on, man. I don't know anyone from Sharon anymore. Not one person.

My friends growing up were all of the nerds from the neighborhood. Like Goofus Carlsberg. Goofus! That's what we called him. I saw the man who walked on the moon at his house. That's a thing you remember. 1969 was a big year! Between space, and riots, and sports, you know, that was an unbelievable year for sports in New York! And the hippie movement. And the liberation of sex. And the liberation of women. And drugs coming out for the first time. When I came to New York, I didn't drink right away. I immediately started smoking pot. And then, in no time, I fucking did acid! The acid they had back then was tremendous. You went to a great place with beautiful backgrounds, and I would just philosophize my whole life: how I came to be as I am, why this is *this*, and why this is *that*. I haven't done acid since 1972, but I did a lot of acid back then. I must have done it 100 times, at least.

But I never even smoked a cigarette in Sharon. I never even had a beer! I was the perfect boy. Never got into trouble. Never started fights. Well, the only fight I ever started… this is a great story. I was like the neighborhood leader, and some little kids came to me and said that a bully was picking on them like crazy. This bully, he was two years younger than me, so they said, "Can you do something about it? Can you beat him up?" I said, "I'll help you guys out. I'll give him a good talking to." So I waited for him at the bus stop and… beat him up. And I'll never forget. I rushed right home. He lived two houses down from me, and his father came racing over in the car. Banging on the door. Ringing and ringing. He screamed, "Your son just beat my son up!" My father wasn't home, but I could hear The Mars from my room: "My son would never do anything like that. He's a nice boy." Everyone hated that family, so it didn't really matter. Everyone. They were just assholes.

I never wanted to be like one of those popular jocks. Yeah, I loved sports, and knew some guys from the teams. I ran track and won a lot of medals, you know, in the Hockamock League. Sharon, Easton, Stoughton, Canton, Foxborough. I ran the 400m, but would always kind of collapse by the end of the race. Those last 50 yards. So junior year, my coach said to me: "Why don't you try the hurdles, man? You could do really well." And I did. I won just about every race during the season. And I won the Hockamock League Championship and went to the class championships. I did lousy there, but figured that senior year I might make State. Anyway, senior year comes around, and I fucked up at the class championships again. I fell on the hurdle. My coach came to me and said, "You fucked up!" I know, man. I hadn't been concentrating. Missed a beat, tripped on the hurdle, and my track career was over.

By that last month of high school, I had switched from training heavily for track to singing in this miserable band.

The only thing good about my band was the name: The Boston Tea Party. We were horrible! My mother would let us practice in the basement, and Bonnie was our biggest fan. She knew we sucked, but I was singing, you know, and playing the tambourine. Steve, the guitar player, lived up the street. He was a genius! Really strange, too, and didn't have many friends. Perfect for me, you know what I mean? And we had a drummer and an organ player, I think. There must have been an organ because I remember doing "96 Tears" by Question Mark and the Mysterians. We played the Monkees, the Beatles, the Stones. Did we have our own songs? I don't think so! We just did covers. Bad covers! All of a sudden, though, girls were hanging around. Younger girls. Bonnie's friends. They were the real reason that I fell on the track.

The group, of course, broke up right after I graduated. Obviously! The drummer, Alan, lived down the street from me. He was one of the cooler guys in the neighborhood. He was like my lieutenant, you know what I mean? I don't want to say anything, but he wasn't too good-looking. We used to make jokes and say we were going to put a curtain in front of him! His father was in the insurance business, so he followed his father and went into the insurance business, too. Ugh! I saw him again back in 1977. This was right after I married Lisa. We had a house on Atlantic Beach and threw this big party. I remember my mother and father came down in a big car. My sister came with her husband Stuey. It was a big thing. And Alan came with his new wife. I hadn't seen him in like ten years. When I knew him back in Sharon, you know, he was really straight. I was really straight then, too, but by 1977, I had done everything!

I told him that we were going into the Village the next day for a big parade. He said, "Okay. We'll go with you. I want to see what Manhattan looks like." So we went into New York and showed them all the major parts of the city. And then I said, "Let's go check out this parade, man." In New York, they were just starting to have these big gay parades. And there were so many gay guys! Shirtless with tattoos and those black caps and everything. Running around all over the place. There were transvestites. There was every kind of person! And he's looking at me like, "What's going on? Where did you take me?" I said, "This is New York, man. It's a parade!" He never spoke to me again.

*

The only bad thing I ever did living in Sharon was take the train downtown to South Station, around Washington Street, and sneak into the sex theater. I did this many times. Back then, in Boston, in the late '60s, they were only showing tits, however, so I was always kind of disappointed.

The first time that I ever saw any kind of anything was at the Brockton Fair. I was like 14 or 15, Bar Mitzvah-ed already. My parents, Bonnie, and I were walking around the fair, but I took off. I split. Because I had heard about this "special" tent! I had to find this tent, man, and I wandered around the fair until I did. There was a guy guarding the entrance, and I was too young to get in. But this wasn't like a little tent. No, this tent was giant, and you could kind of open it up from the bottom. So… I snuck right under. On stage, there was a typical burlesque show like from the '40s and the '50s, you know, comedian and a little band. And then the dancer came out. She only stripped down to like pasties and a bikini, but that was the first time I was ever a part of that ceremony. That ritual. The woman is up on stage. She takes off her clothes. And I'm one of all these guys, the minions below, worshipping her. That's how I looked at it. I always have.

I brought that up to some people recently, and they were like, "Yeah! Yeah! The Brockton Fair! They had a strip show there and everything." So that just sealed it for me. Even before that, though, I used to worship all the voluptuous actresses. They were like goddesses to me. These were women, I thought, who were not stuck in the same rut as everyone else. Housewives. The traditional 1950s *Leave It to Beaver* kind of thing. That was everywhere. And I always found that to be horrible! I loved Marilyn Monroe. She was tremendous, and I cried when she died. And the European actresses: Anita Ekberg, Sophia Loren. And, of course, *Playboy* centerfolds! We used to look for *Playboys* wherever we could find them. One of my friends, his father always had a stash. We'd spread them out all over the room, like 50 centerfolds, and just cover the entire floor!

One time, I remember someone saying, "My father has a stag film! Does anyone have a machine?" Somebody had like an 8mm projector, and we put it on. I bet it was like from the '20s – the roaring '20s! – when film was just beginning. Because there was no talking. The people wore black socks and black masks and nothing else. The women wore masks like they were going to a ball. The men just had like Lone Ranger masks. And then... they had sex. That was my first time ever looking at any kind of actual sex. I thought, "What? This is fucking stupid!" Because they were wearing masks, you know what I mean? I'd rather look at *Playboy* centerfolds! But I don't think my father ever had any *Playboys* in the house. At least, I could never find them! He could've had gangs of them. Who knows? I don't know what he was into. No one in my family ever talked about sex. Never mentioned it. Not one time. Totally repressed! I got all my knowledge from the movies and the streets and everywhere else.

In fact, my father – my father! – during the second semester of my freshman year of college, he came to New York and said, "I want to talk to you about sex." Can you believe that? I said, "Dad! I think we're going to switch positions. I'm going to teach you about sex!" Seriously. Because, that year, I'd learned so much. I went through the whole hippie thing. I'd done acid so many times already. And Quaaludes. And orgies! There were no sex diseases and no one had anything to be scared about. There was no AIDS. There was no nothing. You just got crabs once in a while.

*

I got crabs once. One summer, between my freshman and sophomore years, I hitchhiked across the country with two guys from Sharon and two guys from New York. Our plan was to get out of the East and the Midwest as fast as we could. Go west, man, to like Colorado. The Grand Canyon, you know what I mean? And California. The whole bit. But we stopped in Pennsylvania, and instead of staying for like an hour, or a night, we ended up there for three days! Fights started breaking out between the New Yorkers and the Bostonians. When we reached Indiana, they were fighting more and more. So here we were, going across the country, you know, really getting to hate each other.

Finally, we get to Colorado, and one friend said to me: "I'm jumping out of this car. Do you want to come with me?" And I said, "Yeah! Let's leave these guys. We'll hitchhike, man." This is like 1970. This friend, I forget his real name, but everyone called him "The Schtuppa." So me and The Schtuppa hitchhiked down through New Mexico, to El Paso, down to the border. And then we went to Arizona, Tuscon and Pheonix, back up to the Grand Canyon. We stayed there for a couple of days and hiked down into the canyon. On the way back up, I had to make a lot of water stops. Anyway, for some reason, The Schtuppa rushed ahead of me. Left me alone. I lost him completely! When I got to the top, I met these four people from Switzerland. Three girls and a guy. We got along great, and they were on their way to Las Vegas. They said, "Sleep with us tonight in the tent. And we'll take off to Vegas tomorrow."

The next morning, as we prepared to leave for Vegas, who did I bump into? The Schtuppa. I said, "You fucking asshole! I met these people from Europe. We're going to Vegas. Maybe you can come." So we threw him in the car. And Las Vegas was nothing like it is now. Back then, there was just one little cowboy section and one little strip where the Mob owned a few hotels. None of the flash or the miserable crowds or anything like that. Anyway, we're in Vegas, with our long hair, of course, and around that era, some people really didn't like you if you had long hair. And we're walking across the street, in the crosswalk, and this old man yelled out, "It says DON'T WALK!" I said, "What? Leave me alone, old man. I'm not bothering you." But then he pulled out his sheriff's badge, you know, and The Schtuppa and I just looked at each other. He said, "For being such assholes, I'm taking you straight to the nearest bus stop!"

After that, we went to California and stayed with my cousins in Woodland Hills. All orange groves. Although we only stayed for a day because I really wanted to see San Francisco. We were the first ones to the freeway in the morning. You'd go to the top of the ramp, and if you were there first, then you were first in line for a ride. That's how it went. But there were a bunch of other people hitching that day. We saw these two cute girls and started talking to them. Eventually, a truck pulled over, and I thought for sure that the girls would get picked up instead of us. Because *they were girls*. There was a couple in the truck, however, and they picked me and my friend. We asked the girls: "Do you want to come with us?" So we all climbed in, and there we were, the four of us in the bed of the truck. The next thing you know, one of the girls is pulling out pot. And then we're all taking our clothes off! We had like an orgy in the back of an open-air truck on the way to San Francisco. I tell you, that's the only time I ever did that!

And when I got to San Francisco... I ended up with crabs. They're these little things that get into your hair. Like under your arms and in your eyebrows. But you take some medicine, and they go away.

*

So these are some little early stories that I didn't even really want to talk about yet, but I just bumped right into them. I can't help it. One crosses into another, crosses into another, you know what I mean? And so much of it blurs together. Basically, in the suburbs, the '60s were the same as the '50s. I'm telling you, until I left Sharon, nothing ever changed. I saw this great movie starring Leonardo DiCaprio. It takes place in the 1950s, and he lives in the suburbs, but he desperately wants to go to Paris and become a writer. He goes into the office every day, and everyone is wearing the same clothes. *Revolutionary Road.* That's it! That's the one! And that's how it was.

We wore uniforms in high school! In the winter, you had to wear a school sweater and a sport jacket. Can you imagine that? Every year, I'd say, "It's winter now. Time for my special sweater." As a matter of fact, I remember during my freshman year in college, they had "Jeans Day" where students would rebel by wearing jeans in the quad. That's how repressed everything was before that. It was *brutally repressed.* Like, for me, I'll never forget, when I was living with my second wife Stacy, in New York, and running a company called Coast to Coast. I would take the bus into work, you know, and see all the other guys in their suits and ties. These guys here were probably going to jobs they hate and had to get all dressed up. I'd think, "How did I get so lucky?" And, as a kid, I never even really thought about making movies. I didn't even own a camera. If anything, I wanted to be a writer.

I didn't really start *writing* writing until college. I told you about that paper I wrote! And, of course, in the early '80s, I wrote tons of columns for my girlfriend, Candice. The dominatrix! I had her in different men's magazines, and over a five-year span, must have written like 60 columns. They were all basically about the repression of female sexuality, you know, and then I'd throw in some dominatrix stuff. I was really pushing her. Yeah, I wanted to crossover female power into the mainstream, you know, it's alright to be glamorous and have a brain at the same time. In the old days, if women had a brain, then they were ugly. And if they were good looking, then they were stupid, you know what I mean? To me, that was chauvinistic bullshit. Men have made so many mistakes because of power and greed and ego and insecurity. I felt that way as a kid, but figured it out *heavily* when I went to college. And when I started doing acid, you know, it just came together perfectly!

Plus, I met tremendous people. Artists. Intellectuals. This was during the anti-war period in New York. Every one of my professors was a radical leftist. They all had new ideas and weren't going back to the old ideas, you know what I mean? I went to Adelphi University. Garden City, New York. Tremendous old Yankee town. Ivy everywhere. I had applied to seven schools and got into every one. Here's a great story. I applied to BC because... I don't know. They had a football team. So my parents and I were on a campus visit, sitting in the priest's office. He said, "Do you like the campus? There's a lot of *nice Catholic girls* here." My mother said, "Very nice campus." My father was like, "Yeah, nice campus." BC! Are you kidding me? My father didn't want me to attend a Christian fucking school! And then the priest said, "What did you say your name was again?" Right away, my father yelled, "Cohen!" And the priest's face dropped to the floor!

I was the only one I knew from Sharon who applied to BC. And they actually accepted me! But I picked Adelphi because it was near New York City. I really wanted to go to NYU, but it was in the city. I wasn't going from like king-of-the-nerds directly into the heart of the city. I would have been creamed! *I would have been squashed!* So Adelphi was perfect for me. Great campus. Ten minutes from New York. Couldn't beat it. 1968-1969. The best. Seriously. Those years were so spectacular. I mean, you still had to do your work. I'll tell you, though, after I started getting high and everything, I wanted to learn. Philosophy and history and film. I loved college!

*

Freshman year, though, after first semester, I did almost get booted out of school. I hardly went to class. I got a C⁻ in everything. To be honest, I was wandering around the city half the time. We'd drive to Chinatown at 4:00 in the morning. Or we'd go to White Castle, the burger joint that they made the movies about. Harold and Kumar. Get high and drive around, you know, eating those little burgers. They didn't have White Castles in Sharon. There wasn't anything in Sharon! So when I came home, like for the summer, I would just smoke in my bedroom. Every night, I would get smashed out of my mind and blast The Who's *Who's Next*. My mother would come into my room: "What's that smell?" I'd say, "Ma, it's pot!" The Mars didn't care. As long as I didn't steal things or murder anybody.

We called her The Mars. Everyone in the neighborhood did. We all loved her so much and felt so comfortable around her. All the kids would come over to hang out, and she was like one of the nerds. So we gave her a nerdy name: The Mars. Next thing you know, everyone was calling her that. My friends. Bonnie's friends. Everyone. She was different, you know, not your regular mother. A character. From another planet. The Mars, but with that Boston "r", so it also sounded like "The Mas." It could go either way, I guess. It was just the perfect name for her! She probably hated when I became a hippie and started smoking pot. I don't know. I never really asked her. But she knew how I was, where I was going. She knew that I was anti-war. And she was anti-war! She was always liberal, my mother. Just terrified to do or say anything.

My father was liberal, too, except when he got a little rich. And then, for a while, he thought those Republicans would help him out with his taxes. Typical. By the time I graduated college, he had already switched back to the Democrats. Do you know who was the speaker at my college graduation? Are you ready for this? George. Bush. Senior! At the time, he was some ambassador to somewhere. My father thought it was one of the worst speeches ever. And it was a horrible speech. Typical, horrible, Republican, George Bush speech, you know what I mean? Most people there wanted to throw things at him. I remember, my friend Andrea, she was really pretty with tits *out to here*. She was a wild, wild girl. And brilliant! Those are the kind of women I like: smart and sexually wild at the same time. At graduation, just to rebel, she wore *nothing* underneath her gown!

She lives upstate here in California, but I haven't spoken to her since 1980. I have to admit, I'm not very good at keeping in touch with people. Like my cousin Bobby. He was kind of cool, you know, a hippie lawyer from Hingham. He took cases for poor people, you know, *pro bono*. I last saw him when my father finally graduated from Northeastern. I had brought this blonde who I was dating at the time. Good looking. 5'9". She wasn't a movie actress. She ran a company and also lived in Marina del Rey. That's how we met. I was driving the 30 miles from Marina to my office in Chatsworth, every day, and was freaking out on the freeways! I couldn't do it, man. Something had to happen. As it turned out, our building housed a few other companies, and this girl, Roxanne, she ran one of them. She came up to me and said, "You're the Pussyman, huh? Those are the biggest hits out there."

I told her about my commute, and she said, "I live in Marina, too." So I offered, "Why don't you drive? We'll take my company car. I'll pay for gas. That way, I won't have to drive on the freeways." And... she became my girlfriend for a while. I brought her to Boston for my father's graduation, and when my cousin Bobby met her, he thought she was the most gorgeous thing in history. I think that was the last time I saw Bobby. No. I saw him at the funerals. Right! I get all those years confused. Because my father graduated like a year before he passed away. When he was going for his PhD.

*

In the '90s, when I would come east to visit my parents, all my father did was study. Psychology. More than I ever studied, I'll tell you that. I'd say, "Dad, the Red Sox are on!" And he'd say, "I'm busy. I have to finish this paper." But the Sox were on! I was home in Boston and wanted to watch the game with him. C'mon!

One great thing about my father, he always took me to sporting events. We had Patriots season tickets. This is when the Patriots played in Fenway Park, you know, before they moved to Foxborough. I remember leaving at halftime because it was so cold. And we went to a ton of Red Sox games. The Celtics, every now and then. I never remember going to a Bruins game. Ever. I've been to a Kings game out here in L.A. It was tremendous! And I hate hockey, you know, but being down low, in the 3rd row, then you see the whole game. Watching it on television, I can't see a thing. Where's the puck? Where's the puck? Goal! Really? The Rangers are the only hockey team that I really like. I watched them when I first moved to New York. I don't know why. They only won one time. 1994. And I already had left! So when I was there, for all of those years, they never won anything at all.

I told you, though, in 1969, my first year in New York, the Jets won, the Mets won, and the Knicks won. Those teams had never won anything before! It's unbelievable. Think about it. The Jets won the Super Bowl when Joe Namath told everyone it was going to happen. And then the Mets won the World Series. The Miracle Mets! And the Knicks won the NBA championship when Willis Reed hobbled into the 7th game. They had Earl "The Pearl" Monroe and Walt "Clyde" Frazier. Clyde was the man in New York. Oh yeah! He was spectacular. Passer. Shooter. Fast. Great defense. Everything! Clyde, Clyde, Clyde was the guy, man. There was no doubt it. Walking around town in his fancy mink coats. Joe Namath, well, he was the biggest. He had this famous club where all of the huge movie stars would hang out. But right there next to Joe Namath was Walt "Clyde" Frazier.

See, I've always loved sports. Forever. My whole life, I've had this personal conflict where I think, "Why am I wasting my time watching these stupid sports?" I've probably asked myself that question 50,000 times. And since the big HDTVs came out, I really watch a lot of sports. Some people warned me: "You're such a sports fanatic. You think you watch games now? You're going to get so hooked!" And they were right. Once I got the big TV, I care more about watching games than just about anything. Maybe it's because I'm a voyeur. I like to watch! I idolize masculine talent, you know, the big sports stars. And I idolize feminine talent, the big-titted actresses. I always say, you know, I'm some combination of male and female. More male, of course. Like 75% male. Maybe 65% and 35%? I mean, I'm no Bruce Jenner!

CHAPTER 3

VOLUNTEERS OF AMERICA

Okay. Where are we? Where are we going? I don't remember.
I have to tell you, in my high school years, not much happened.
Really. But as soon as I got to New York and wandered around
downtown and throughout the Village, I couldn't believe how
many hippies there were! It was like San Francisco. There
were so many hippies. Yeah, I had seen them in Cambridge,
but they weren't like in *droves*. They were in droves! That
flipped me out, man. These people with their crazy outfits,
colorful and different, you know what I mean? I loved it all. I
was like, "Wow! Everything is beginning!"

I always wanted to move to San Francisco. Since I was
17 years old and first read about Haight-Ashbury, I thought,
"Ultimate Freedom City! San Francisco!" I never did move
there because of the earthquakes. Not for me, man! But
you didn't have to be in San Francisco to be a part of the
counterculture. It was everywhere. Everyone was listening
to the San Francisco bands. I loved Jefferson Airplane. They
had a great female singer, Grace Slick, and they talked about
everything that was happening. Their big album *Volunteers*
was about the whole anti-war movement and having a
revolution. No one plays it anymore. Nobody even knows
about it anymore! I was dying to go to San Francisco. And
if I couldn't live in San Francisco, and I couldn't because of
the earthquakes, then New York was my second choice. I
had to leave Sharon, man, and explore. You know what that's
about. Exploring.

In New York, the hippies would hang out down at the
Fillmore East. I saw everybody there. Jefferson Airplane, the
Moody Blues, Frank Zappa and the Mothers of Invention.

They would have three tremendous bands on the same night for five bucks. I remember seeing Led Zeppelin there right after they put out their very first album. If you can believe it, they were the second group on the bill. Iron Butterfly was the headliner, you know, they had that song "In-A-Gadda-Da-Vida." You ever hear that song? It sucks, but was a giant hit on every board in the world. When Zeppelin came on, though, the whole place exploded! They played a tremendous set, and everyone was like, "Don't leave! Don't leave!" You know what I mean? So, yeah, pretty much everyone played there at the Fillmore. Everyone except for the Rolling Stones or the Beatles. Groups like that.

I did see the Beatles once. They came to Suffolk Downs in 1966 on their one tour through Boston. One of Bonnie's friends had an extra ticket, so I tagged along with my sister and her friends. I didn't care, man. A lot of guys were jealous of the Beatles because the girls liked them so much. I remember seeing *Hard Days Night* in the theater, and you couldn't hear anything. The girls just screamed the entire movie! And that's what happened at the concert. As a matter of fact, as we were walking out, I remember some girl yelling, "Did anyone actually see George Harrison? I was too far back." I said, "Yeah, I saw him." And she said to *me*, "Can I have an autograph?" What? I'm not George Harrison! I'm just some guy who went to the concert. I'll never forget that. That's how fanatical they were about the Beatles.

Actually, the first time I got laid was with one of Bonnie's friends. A non-Jew. I went with a non-Jew in the Jewish town. I was rebelling! What was her name? I went on a visit to New York for – what's it called? – orientation! This was probably in June after I graduated high school. And I was so excited. I thought, "Wow! I'm finally going to get laid in New York, right?" But I came back to Sharon for the summer, and Bonnie introduces me to… Kathy! Blonde. 5'7". Really smart. And just a little nymphomaniac. She wanted sex all the time. And so did I. Of course! I was 18. That whole summer, we had so much sex. Outside at Sharon Lake. My house. Her house.

Kathy was my only steady girlfriend before college. I went out with a number of other girls, but I was a virgin up until that summer. But then I went to New York and forget about it. I became different.

In high school, though, everywhere I could, I read about the hippies in San Francisco and New York and any kind of liberation from the stagnant existence that society forces upon us as human beings. I was already planning, man. Free love! Free expression! And I had been to New York already. When I was 16 years old, my parents took me there, and we stayed in a big hotel and went to a Broadway play. We were supposed to go the United Nations, too, but – guess what? – I got a sore throat. I've been getting these awful sore throats since I was a kid. I'm probably DNA-ed in this area! I'm sick all the time, you know, so I like to complain. How could I be Jewish and not complain? At the dog park, I'll complain to other people, and they complain to me. Some of them, if they're from New York and can take a joke, I'll give them shit. People from the West Coast will sometimes get a little sensitive. I'll say, "Don't worry about it, man. I'm just fucking fooling around!"

New Yorkers are different. When I lived in New York, the guys there would give each other shit. Constantly. That's New York, you know what I mean? It's got its own particular thing going on. From that first time I visited, I knew that I wanted to be there. So by the end of my freshman year, that second semester, that was it for me! I really changed radically and became an alternative lifestyle person. Running around. Rock n' roll clubs. Sex theaters. That's what I really cared about. I would hop on the train and go to a porno movie once a week. And now, they were real porno movies, you know, so I was happy!

*

I was a History major in college. I was into the early 20th century, 1900 to 1914, then WWI to the depression, WWII. Some European history. And ancient history! I was always digging, you know, trying to figure things out. I saw how this is basically a patriarchal society that we've been living in forever, and that somehow, through history, men have reversed the natural ways of the universe. And I realized right away that the corporations were taking over this country. Big time! I read about Eisenhower and his famous statement: "Watch out for the Industrial Complex. Military Complex. And the corporations. Together. Look out for them." No one has listened. No one remembers. Only people like me. Big leftists. Well, I don't know if I'd call myself a leftist. I'm basically an independent. A free thinker. That's what I am.

It was an exciting time to be in college. We were against that bastard Nixon, you know what I mean? We weren't supposed to be in Vietnam! And I was in danger of being drafted. Well, my first year in college, there was a rule: if you were a student, then you were exempt. They took that rule away, though, when they expanded the war, and I was thrown into the draft. My number was six over the cut-down. Let's say, if the cut-down was like 240, then I was like 246. So I didn't have to go, but I was thinking all these things: *Maybe I'll go to Canada? Maybe I'll fake being gay?* Anything to not fucking go! One person I knew went to Vietnam: my friend Lenny. He got malaria over there, and shot up with shrapnel, and came back a heavy radical. My sophomore year, Nixon sent the National Guard onto to the campuses. Reagan did it first out here in California. When he was the governor, you know, he sent the military to Berkeley. And then Kent State happened.

What happened is Nixon expanded the war from Vietnam into Cambodia. He was trying for all French Indochina: Cambodia, Laos, Vietnam. The French were in control there for years and years. After WWII, the French said they would leave and they left, but we came along. There was that fake boat attack. Gulf of Tonkin. Lyndon Johnson said one of our ships was attacked, you know, but it never happened. Never happened! And they killed Kennedy. I was 14 years old, and I remember walking through the school corridors and hearing that Kennedy was shot. That afternoon, I went bowling... by the way, did you know that bowling is now really popular here in Los Angeles? Bowling? I'm shocked! I haven't bowled since high school. In Massachusetts, we used to have candlepins. We were the only state! When I tell people from other parts of the country about candlepin bowling, you know, those little balls, they look at me like, "What are you talking about?"

What am I talking about? Kennedy! Right! So when my mother picked me up at the bowling alley, she was crying. Everyone was crying. Even as a young person, conspiracy theorist that I am, I saw the whole thing. He went to Dallas, you know, Texas, a place where they hated him, and Johnson was this big honcho. And then Johnson was on the plane with him going back as the new president. I thought, "Kennedy wasn't assassinated by this fucking patsy. He was killed by Johnson and his gang." I told everyone, but they were all like, "No way! Are you kidding? Our own government wouldn't shoot the president." Yeah right! Of course they would! They'd kill anyone! That's pretty obvious. Since then, I've always known that our government is not the great democracy that it's made out to be. The whole country, you know, is totally fucked. Especially since Dick Cheney. He fucked everything! On purpose! And I could see that happening even back then, you know what I mean?

I never became a commune hippie or anything, but I went to all the college demonstrations. And I remember being tear-gassed at Yale. My friends and I made the drive to New Haven. We were holding signs and yelling, and the National Guard was there, shooting pellets and tear-gassing everyone. And we ran! That's what I remember. Running!

*

At that time, the campuses were really rampaging, and we were always demonstrating. During my sophomore year, the teachers walked out of their classes and joined the students.

They led the students! You know what I got for grades in school that year? Straight A's across the board. I went from almost flunking out my freshman year to straight A's. Because I didn't have to go to class! I remember calling up my mother up and saying, "Ma, this is the greatest semester ever!"

That's also the same year that I took my first film classes, learned some basic filmmaking, and even made a few little movies. These were basic little anti-war movies, you know, and I had no idea what I was doing. There was one where we made this whole big production of taking down the American flag from the student center. I don't know. I didn't really understand anything about film yet. But I learned. That's why I was able to direct when I finally got the opportunity. I started out as a performer, you know, but never ever wanted to be an actor. I wanted to be a director! As an actor, you can't really promote your own vision. You can only interpret someone else's vision. And I had this big plan to push the power of pussy! Power of the woman! I'm not Bruce Jenner, but I've always had that inside of me.

Of course, there wasn't any sex in my anti-war movies. Back then, they would keep those things kind of separate. Unless it was a big movie like *Easy Rider*, you know what I mean? *Easy Rider* came out in 1969 and was humongously influential. I remember being like, "Wow! This is the real deal, man!" The whole idea was so powerful to me. Doing what you want. Not going into the office every day from 9:00-5:00 where you have to wear the same clothes. Freedom! In the '70s, movies in general went through this total transformation where they really became a powerful way of communicating. That's when all the big American directors started out. These guys who are now over 70 years old: Scorsese, Coppola, Di Palma. Lucas and Spielberg. They all knew each other. Half of them went to film school here at USC.

And Mike Nichols. He did *The Graduate*, but that was the '60s. As a matter of fact, I went on a date to see *The Graduate* with some girl who lived in Sharon. I can't remember her name. I only remember Kathy. In college, though, I had some other steady girlfriends. Junior and senior year, you know, I had a girlfriend named Lori, and we actually thought about getting married. She was a Jew from Long Island who liked to start fights with me in Macy's. I hate shopping, so I'd say, "Okay, okay, let's do something else already." And she would start screaming at me right in the middle of the store! I was like, "What is this yelling in public about?" And then I visited her house to meet her family, and I'll tell you, the father never stopped screaming. He's yelling at the mother! The mother's yelling back! Lori's yelling! They're all screaming at each other! It made sense. Here was this big, tough, abusive guy, trying to be a big shot because he's insecure. And this is the way he takes it out on the other people in the house, you know, his wife and daughter.

But I went with her for a while. When I was working at State Beef over the summers, every couple of weeks, I would drive to New York and stay with Lori for days at a time. My father would get so pissed! He wanted me in Boston, you know, working at State Beef the whole time. In those days, I didn't mind driving. Now, I never drive! Because of my back more than anything. My back is so fucked up! I've been to an orthopedic guy, but I refuse to have the surgery. I've seen too many disasters and heard too many horror stories. That's why Bruce Jenner… I'm sorry, Caitlyn Jenner. Changing your sex is a really difficult *torturous* thing to do. I know the person already feels kind of tortured because they're not in the right body, but how many operations do they need? Six? Seven? Ten? Probably 20! And then, you know, they have to cut their dick off and make it into a whole new thing.

So I don't know why I brought up Caitlyn Jenner. I have no idea. Anyway, I still went out with Lori after college, but we finally broke up. It turned out that my second wife, Stacy, was sort of like her, you know, another strong Jew from Long Island. And my first wife, Lisa, was also Jewish, but from New Jersey, so she was a little different. And there were so many other girls before Lori. Like Andrea, the one who walked naked at graduation. She was my best friend, so we had sex a lot. That's the way it was back then. Especially after you took Quaaludes. They didn't cost anything and were *legal*. Right over the counter. Remember my friend, The Schtuppa? He worked part-time in a pharmacy and could get us whatever we wanted. And once we took Quaaludes, everyone would start having sex. Man, we had a lot of swinging parties! The next morning, you wouldn't really remember exactly which woman you did or anything. I mean, you'd know what was going on while you were doing it, but the next morning… nothing. That's how that drug was. It was wacky!

And if you watch the movie that Scorsese just made, *The Wolf of Wall Street*, they were so out of control doing drugs. They did coke all over the place, you know, and then, all of a sudden, they pulled out some Quaaludes. And I hadn't even heard the word Quaaludes in 30 years! Because they outlawed them in like the mid '80s. In the movie, though, these guys do so many! At first, they do two, and nothing happens, so they do two more. Finally, they take a fifth one and they can't move at all, you know what I mean? They're plopping on the ground, foaming from the mouth. It's DiCaprio and – what's his name? – Jonah Hill. He's tremendous! His best performance ever. He makes the movie. He really does.

*

This is when the real porno movies were just starting, so once a week, I would go to the sex theater. For the first time ever, I got to see the whole thing. I was like, "Yes! Finally! Freedom!" Most people, though, didn't want to go with me. They didn't care about porno movies. I did! That was me. I wanted to see female genitalia. And the first movies that came out were called "San Francisco Beavers." They weren't really even movies. There would be like 15 different scenes of one woman playing with herself. Masturbating. And I'd watch them over and over and over. Maybe I'd fantasize about being down there, eating her out. I would even think, "That might be a pretty good job. To be a stripper. Or in the movies."

That's when I first became aware of the sex business. After college, my mother asked me: "So what are you going to do?" I didn't get my master's degree right away. I lived back in Boston for one year and worked at State Beef. While I was home, I sent out applications and then began a program the following September. That's when I told my father: "Don't count on me at State Beef anymore." I wanted to become a teacher. But it was always in the back of my mind, you know, if I don't teach, then the sex business sounds pretty exciting. Some of those early movies were like huge mainstream hits! For a few years there, everyone was talking about *Deep Throat*. Even more so after Watergate. That movie made millions and millions of dollars. People would stand in line at the theaters, you know, around the block. Even couples went to see *Deep Throat*. Oh yeah. That's how big it was.

As it turned out, Gerard Damiano was the first guy that I ever did a sex scene for. I told you, I was doing tons of PA work. Schlepping equipment and that kind of stuff. Well, I somehow wound up on a Gerry Damiano shoot, this famous guy who directed *Deep Throat*. After that, he did *The Devil in Miss Jones*, one other picture, and then this movie, you know, that I was hired on as a PA. It was called *Portrait* and starred a woman named Jody Maxwell from Kansas City. I think she met Damiano at a lecture at the University of Arizona. Because of the success of *Deep Throat*, he would lecture across the country about sexuality. He was like this big celebrity! So they were talking, and she told him that she could do this trick. She said, "I can suck two cocks at the same time while I hum, 'How Much Is That Doggie in the Window?'" She performed that trick for him, and he hired her on the spot. He gave her the name Jody Maxwell, "The Singing Cocksucker from Kansas City."

So I'm going to be a PA on *this set*. Two days before we start shooting, my friend Michael, who happened to be doing the lighting for this picture, he said to me: "Gerry told me that one of the guys is not going to make it, and he needs a replacement. How about it? I think you would be perfect!"

And I said, "What are you talking about? I've never done a porno movie." But I was really interested – of course! – so I went to speak with Damiano. He asked me, "So you've never done a scene in a movie before?" I told him, "Don't worry about a thing! I've been on many sets. No problem. I'll carry this scene *easily*." I had been on a shitload of sets by then. Maybe 20 or 30. I don't know. But porno sets? Only a couple. I had mostly worked on commercials, you know what I mean? Anyway, that's what I told him. I said, "Don't worry about a thing!" And he said, "Okay. You've got the job."

And this was the job: I walk into a bathroom while Jody Maxwell is reading on the toilet, and she sees me, gives me a blowjob, and I'm supposed to cum. That's it. That's it? To me, this sounded pretty nerve-racking. I wasn't used to having sex in a bathroom! Also, in those days, I was used to hippie girls. They weren't concerned about makeup, you know, or tight little dresses. They didn't shave under their arms or anything. They were fucking hippies! So I get on the set, and Jody Maxwell is probably ten years older than me. She's dressed in a corset like *The Best Little Whorehouse in Texas*. I walked into that bathroom and... I just came. Immediately. Before I even got a full hard-on! I thought to myself, "I blew it. I'm finished." I told Damiano that I could do it easily and I fucked up. So I'm walking out really depressed, and he approached me. He said, "I'll tell you what. You seem like a good kid. I'm going to give you another chance. We'll break for lunch, and when we come back, I'll take you out of the bathroom, put you on a bed, and see what happens."

And the rest is history.

*

Here's a quick lesson in how the porno business began. It's really a chapter in itself, but here we go. At first, there were these little pocketbooks. Some didn't even have pictures, just dirty stories, you know what I mean? And some had black and white pictures of like ugly, old strippers. And there were also these nudist camp books. In the '60s, I guess, there was some fascination with nudist camps. When I saw these books, I thought they were horrible! They showed naked people like playing volleyball, you know, never in suggestive poses of any kind. The people were not good looking. Not sexy at all! I didn't know why they were selling like wild.

So there were the little pocketbooks and the nudist camp books and they were sold in bookstores. That's why they called them: adult *bookstores*. The books were produced by the Printers, the same people that printed other kinds of material: comic books, pulp fiction, adventure magazines. These Printers realized that their sex books were outselling everything else by 50 times! They contacted the other Printers, you know, the printer in Cleveland, the printer in L.A., and they said, "We're making a ton! You want to join in with this printing? We'll expand from here." So they decided to go into the movie business. They went to their friends *who were Italian*, who they had grown up with in Brooklyn, and that's how the business got going. These Jewish printers with Italian backing for muscle. And they got lucky with the hippies. It was hippies, you know, who made the original movies. Now, you actually had all these people who were more than willing to get naked and have sex on camera.

This is an era where people were engaging in totally new forms of sexual expression. And even when I started being in the movies, I didn't call it pornography. I thought of them as "freedom sex movies." Everything fit together. It all began with the anti-war movement, and then the sexual revolution, and from there, the women's revolution. Because women were completely repressed. Women, nowadays, they don't realize what others went through to get to the point where we are now. I know, most of the movies were directed by men and presented a man's vision. Yeah, that's mostly true. But my idea was to work my way into the business and eventually put my own kind of ideas forward. That was always my goal: to change things for the good. Make love, not war, you know what I mean? The Vietnam War, like the Iraq War, just went on forever. It went from like 1965 to 1975. A whole decade! We were fighting over there that whole time, man.

Meanwhile, so many cultural changes were happening. Clothing and music and sex. We started questioning religion. We started *questioning*. People had stopped questioning. You never stop questioning! Ever! If you stop questioning, then that's the end! I'm always questioning. Wanting to learn. Even though I can't remember a lot of things anymore, I still like to learn a little something every day.

*

You see, there really was no sex business when I first got to New York. But then, like I said, those little 8mm movies started coming out of San Francisco. And they were always hippies. Because who else would do it? You could get prostitutes, but they weren't allowed on the sets. Now, half of the actresses are also prostitutes because the business is so bad. Not all the girls, but a number of them. *Escorts*. They don't call them prostitutes anymore. And when they become known in the movies, then it's easier to book gigs in the strip clubs. For a while there, in the late '80s, girls would do a few movies just to get on a box cover. When I ran Coast to Coast, I would pick the girls for the box covers. So that was a good job!

That's where I met my friend Bruce/Will Divide. He was a salesman for Coast to Coast and actually the one who pushed me to make *Pussyman*. At that point, I had stopped directing completely. I just didn't have enough time and energy in New York because I was running this company. But after Bruce/Will Divide and I came out to Los Angeles… boom! Okay. This is the early '90s. I just jumped ahead 20 years! I made the first *Pussyman* movie for Coast to Coast, and it sold 150,000 copies. It did unbelievable. It went to #1. We shot one huge four-hour movie and then divided it in two. Like Quentin Tarantino did with *Kill Bill*. We thought, "Wow! What a great idea! Let's just make this giant fucking movie, then divide it in half." Will Divide! He got that name from a city sign. We were walking around New York, and on one of the buildings, we read: WILL DIVIDE. And he said, "Wow! What a great name!" And I said, "Yeah! Yeah! That's your name."

He moved out to L.A. before me and learned how to be a producer. And then I followed shortly after. That's when all these people wanted to back me, you know, so I finally left New York. I always had this vision that I was going to be a special communicator and communicate the power of female sexuality. I just had a premonition that this is what I was supposed to do. What I wanted to do, either through movies or books or becoming a college lecturer, is somehow communicate the idea that sexuality, for a woman, is a good thing. That if she orgasms, it's a great thing! And to do whatever I could to help humans get over the repression and guilt that I grew up with. So when the *Pussyman* movies came out, and they were so unbelievably popular, I was ecstatic. Between '93 and '97, I made a total of 15 *Pussyman* pictures. But that was my goal from the very beginning.

The first picture I ever directed was called *Secluded Passion*. 1984. I wrote the script and everything. What I tried to do was switch the traditional male and female roles. You had to be pretty intellectual to pick it up, you know, but there were little hints everywhere. In the movie, I live with my sister who forces me to go out and get a job. She sends me over to this strip club where men dance for women. And I get hired. By Candice, my girlfriend at the time, the dominatrix. She's the owner of the club. It was a really good movie! I actually lost my only copy, but recently, a fan of mine, some 50-year old woman, messaged me through Facebook. She said, "I've loved your movies for 25 years." And then she said that she owned a copy of *Secluded Passion*. I said, "Wow! That's the first movie I ever directed. I don't even have that!" Guess what? It arrived in the mail a week later.

I don't know how I got us to that story. What was the question you asked me? I'm skipping all over the joint!

CHAPTER 4
SOME LIKE IT HOT

In New York, living at the beach, we were such big hippies that we didn't even have a television. We did not believe in being influenced by the networks. And there were no computers, so if you didn't have a television, then that was it, man. For a few years, though, my friends and I would rent a huge television to watch the NBA playoffs. The biggest television in the store! We'd keep it for the whole playoffs and then return it. We didn't care about anything else.

I remember watching Game 5 of the 1976 NBA Finals. You've heard about this game, right? The Celtics and the Suns. At the beginning of the series, I really thought that the Celts were going to sweep Phoenix. They had the great John Havlicek, Dave Cowens, Paul Silas. And Jo Jo White! He was on that team and he was tremendous! So this was just an unbelievable game that went to triple overtime. I'll never forget, it was on tape delay. The game had already happened, but I didn't know who won. Not like today, you know, where you can put on ESPN and instantly see every score. We thought Havlicek had won the game in the first overtime. He banked in a runner at the buzzer. There we were at the beach, screaming our heads off, jumping up and down. In Boston, at the Garden, all the fans stormed the floor. It was chaos!

As it turned out, there was still one second left, and they had to get everybody off the court. Phoenix then made this crazy shot to tie the game, but the Celts finally won, *two overtimes later*. One of the best basketball games in history! That's when I was a Celtics fanatic. Big time! I was into the Celtics almost as much as the Red Sox. And I still like the Celtics, you know, but – it's kind of strange – I like the

Lakers just as much. Maybe even a bit more. I used to *hate* the Lakers, you know what I mean? More than any other team! And recently, when the Celtics played the Lakers in the Finals, two years in a row, I would have my friends over to watch the games. Most of them are Lakers fans. Except for Mike Graffone, of course, because he grew up in Boston like me. Anyway, I was in a room full of people rooting for the Lakers and I kept saying, "Hey, I can't go wrong." If the Celtics win: fine! If the Lakers win: great! Put those teams in the Finals every year, man. I can't lose!

*

Obviously, growing up, we had a television. We were actually the first ones in the neighborhood to get a color TV, and all the kids would come over to our house on Sunday nights to watch Disney's *Wonderful World of Color*. This is like at the beginning, you know, when color TV was just on Sundays. So that was a big night! And *Bonanza* was in color. My favorite shows growing up were the Westerns. Cowboy shows. *Gunsmoke* and *Have Gun Will Travel*.

I remember through, always, even when I was like six or seven years old, if I saw a show with a voluptuous woman, then I'd be interested! I'll never forget this one episode of *The Honeymooners*. Jackie Gleason was with Art Carney, and his friend came over with his wife, and this wife was one of these voluptuous women, you know, tight dress, all over. Jackie Gleason and Art Carney, they couldn't keep their heads on straight. Their tongues fell out of their mouths. They couldn't talk or anything. They were just flabbergasted by a woman like this. And those were the kind of women that I loved! Like the James Bond girls, you know, *Goldfinger* came out in 1964. Same year as the Beatles. Exact same month. "I Want to Hold Your Hand" and "She Loves You" were released in February of '64. And then, "From Me to You / Please Please Me" shortly after. The Beatles had the top three songs on the chart. And then *Goldfinger* came out a week or two after that.

I loved *Goldfinger*. Pussy Galore! She was a woman in the movie who worked for the bad guys, but she met up with James Bond, played by Sean Connery. Of course, every woman loved Sean Connery. So they went to bed. They didn't actually show it, you know, but they showed them together. And the next shot, you see her, naked, covered in gold paint. That's how they killed her. They covered her pores with paint. At that time, "pussy" wasn't something people really said. Not at all. I mean, yeah, it was a slang term for the vagina, but it was a small term. Not used very often. And the word "pussy" being for a guy, you know, not being tough, that wasn't really used either. I think the word "pussy" might have become big after *Goldfinger*. Who knows? Because, now, people say "pussy" all the time!

Those James Bond movies were so huge and – to me – very influential. There was also *A Shot in the Dark* with Peter Sellers and Elke Sommer, part of the *Pink Panther* series. I remember they go to a nudist camp in that one! Another movie from that time period was this big comedy starring Jack Lemmon called *Under the Yum Yum Tree*. Jack Lemmon played this Hollywood landlord who only rented to sexy single women. I remember loving that movie. Because there were like 50 women in it! And, of course, even before that, *Some Like It Hot* with Jack Lemmon and Tony Curtis. Running around in drag. Hiding from the Mob. Meanwhile, they're chasing after this big sexpot played by Marilyn Monroe. That was tremendous! As a kid, I must have watched that movie 20 times, every time it was on. Later, I actually bought my own copy on cassette. I still have it, you know, somewhere over there by the TV.

*

We selected our own shows, Bonnie and I, and The Mars would sit there with us. She let us put on whatever we wanted. My father, of course, would be sleeping. Out like a light. He got up for work, you know, at like 3:00 in the morning. And when he got home, he'd have three or four Scotches and be totally ripped! And then he would eat, sit around for half an hour, and pass out. Every day. My mother never touched alcohol. Every now and then, she would have milk with a little drop of Kahlúa. That was it. And she would get *pissed* if they went to a party or something and my father got smashed. She would yell, "You're making a fool of yourself!" My father liked to drink. So what? He worked so fucking hard! Let the guy have a good time here and there.

This was a standard thing for people in the '60s. The man comes home from work, has a few cocktails, his wife brings him some food, and then he passes out. And how we ate was tremendous! My father would get his meal first, you know, and immediately start eating. I'd get my food second, and then Bonnie after me. While my mother was still in the kitchen, we would race to see who could finish the fastest. My father set the pace, and we followed his lead. Remember, too, this was mostly lousy food. As a cook, you know, The Mars was bottom of the line. So we would just wolf it all down! My father always won the race because he had that head start. And he would eat so fast! He was starving. He probably hadn't eaten anything during the day, running all around the meat market. He never went for lunch. Ever. He was always working. Totally fucking focused.

Yeah, he was just an unbelievably focused person. That's how he kept himself in such great shape. I remember him doing those calisthenics, you know, push-ups and sit-ups and stretches. After he retired, he had this whole regimen. On one day, he would go to the gym, do calisthenics, or run on the track. On another day, he'd swim a hundred laps. Really. I saw him do it. Out at the pool where they lived when they moved into that condo in Waltham. He told me he could swim a hundred laps, and I said, "C'mon, dad. No way." I can't swim a hundred laps! But he did. You know, he had a heart attack in his 30s, back when I was like three years old. While he was building a big fence around the house. I don't remember it at all. Zero recollection. But I was told that, you know, when I was older. It mustn't have been a very bad one, I guess, because he continued doing everything!

If I really had a lot of Abe in me, then I would be focused in business like him. I'd be able to forget about everything else and just do my thing. But I can't. Especially when I started working from my house. I thought it would be great, you know, not going into the office anymore. I found out, though, when I'm at home, I just think about everything else but work: dog, *this, that*, you know what I mean? I'm so scattered, man. That's why I haven't written this book already. Because I can't focus and do it myself. I can talk for hours and hours, but to actually put it down on paper? Yeah, I have that A.D.D. and definitely didn't get it from my father. My sister wasn't A.D.D. She took more after my father, and I took more after my mother. Bonnie was descended from Abe, and I was descended from The Mars.

My mother was so sweet, but she gave me some bad things, man. She was a notorious worrier and petrified of everything. And she always needed someone to protect her. I don't always need someone to protect me, but it's nice to have a tough person around. *Tougher than me!* And that's why I always have these panic attacks. She panicked all the time! Often, while driving, and then we'd have to take her to the hospital. I remember, when we were still living in Sharon, and she was driving to the South Shore Mall in Braintree. She got a ticket for going *too slow* on the highway, you know, 20mph under the speed limit! And if my father got home an hour late from work, she'd go bananas and call up every person she knew. When I hitchhiked across the country, and she didn't hear from me for a few days, she called everyone. Friends. Family. Even the State Police! You can't call the State Police to look for a guy who is hitchhiking! A hippie-looking guy like me! Are you kidding?

Oh God. Jewish neurotics. Worried about everything in the world. And I have tons of that. I can't control it! It's in my DNA, you know what I mean? No doubt about it. Like this sore throat thing that I've had forever. I think I was born with it. I was born an "inky," you know, just 2.5 lbs., a few weeks early, and had to be kept in the incubator. And I was a Cesarean. So I have this joke that the reason why I love pussy so much, why I'm so *obsessed*, you know, is that I never came out the right way. Could be! I'm trying to get back to the origin. The original hole. It's all about holes, man.

*

I got along with my father, *but I didn't*. We would argue about everything. I was always rebelling, you know, and I think he really wanted me to take over State Beef. Fathers always want their sons to go into the same business as them. It's been like that forever.

As a matter of fact, at the company I ran in New York, Coast to Coast, my boss hired one of his sons to be a salesman. The son did nothing! He'd come in at like 11:00am. Play games. Talk on the phone. Why did I bring him up? Right! Fathers and sons. So my boss said to my friend Bruce/Will Divide: "You'll have a piece of the company when we're done." And I warned Bruce/Will Divide: "No way, man. He'll give the business to the sons. You ain't gonna get shit." And that's what happened. At the time, I was running one of his companies, and my wife Stacy was running an associate company. We were always invited to his family affairs. And I'll never forget, he came to us many times and said, "You'll be taken care of forever. If you stay with us, then you're set for life." I knew right away that he was lying.

The people that we were working for, I found out later, they were like the Mob. Part of the Mob, anyway. *Affiliated* with the Mob. Certain sections of the Mob, you know, were involved in the porno business, and that's who I worked for at Coast to Coast. So it was kind of exciting! One time, I went to see this producer to go over some scripts. When I arrived at his office, there was this guy who kind of looked like muscle, but also not, dressed in like a $10,000 suit. This guy ended up being killed by Sammy "The Bull" Gravano, the famous mobster who knocked off a boss outside some steakhouse in Manhattan. That was big news in New York, and that's when John Gotti became the big boss. Before then, Gotti was just a foot soldier, but he shot his way to the top. And Sammy "The Bull" was then one of the informants who helped the FBI nail Gotti. I don't know the actual infrastructure of how they do it, you know, but they all just kill each other and fuck each other over.

The Mob ran the porno business in New York for decades. And I remember a few people in the business who just disappeared. Personally, I think they were probably "taken care of," you know what I mean? Thrown in the water somewhere, never to be seen again. They probably tried to steal a little money or something and got themselves killed. That's why, when I moved out to Los Angeles, I didn't tell my boss that I was coming out to shoot movies. I told him that I was on vacation. I had made those first two *Pussyman* movies for Coast to Coast, but my plan was to come out here and start my own company. Maybe I would go back and forth, try to do both, but we couldn't reach a deal. Instead, he actually started this other line with Randy West, a big porn star at the time, and went into direct competition with *Pussyman*. Both lines were being made by the same company! But his new line flopped completely, and *Pussyman* went on to become one of the most popular series in porn history!

So, in September of '94, I came out to California on a three-week vacation, and we shot these huge fucking movies, *Pussyman 3* and *Pussyman 4*. I mean, giant mansions and tons of everything. They probably were like $100,000 movies, which in porn is a decent amount. And on video. We didn't shoot on film anymore. And then, at the end of my vacation, I called him up from California and said, "Hey, I quit. I'm starting my own *Pussyman* company out here." If I had made that move ten years earlier, you know, then they probably would have come out here and done something to me. That was a dangerous move I made. Okay. I did have some balls once in a while!

*

The business went to video in 1983. That's when the budgets shrunk, and they started to allow a few actors to become directors. Really, there were only two of us at the time. Me and Ron Jeremy.

Ron Jeremy was the first actor to travel the country from San Francisco to New York to Los Angeles. So everyone knew him! He was always pushing himself to become a big Hollywood movie star. He'd brag about getting little scenes in these real movies. He'd say, "Hey, guess what? I'm in *Ghostbusters*." And I'd say, "Where are you in *Ghostbusters*, Ron? I watched the whole movie." And he'd say, "Oh, I was the one in the crowd. In that section *there*." Very good. He was part of the 100,000 people in the crowd. I don't call that a role! But I guess he did kind of make himself known to everyone. He's the same age as me, you know, and he grew up in Whitestone, New York, the town where Stacy and I were living before I moved out here. And he was going to be a teacher, too. He got his master's degree and everything.

He and I have a lot in common, but unlike me, he really wanted to be an actor. And a comedian! I remember, there was a private party for Al Goldstein, the head of *Screw*, this big weekly magazine in New York. They advertised for hookers and had like local alternate lifestyle stories. So there, in some club they had rented for the night, Ron went up on stage and started to do his act. And people threw stuff at him because he was so bad! That was a thing. It was like a running joke. Make fun of Ron. He'd come to a set, eat all the food he could find, and be on the phone the entire time. I'd be screaming at him: "Get over here! Do this! Do that!" Because I would put him in all the movies I directed in New York. And he would put me in all the pictures he directed. We had a deal, you know, but what a pain in the ass he was!

We'll leave Ron Jeremy soon, but I have to tell you a quick little funny story. The first time I met him, we were at a casting call together in New York. Sitting there in the office, waiting and talking, he said to me: "I can do something no one else can do. I can suck my own cock." What? That's what he said! "I can suck my own cock." And, sure enough, we both got hired for that movie. Three weeks later, we were shooting in some theater, and he walked right up on stage... and just did it. No kidding! I mean, he was skinny when he first started acting. When you see him now, you know, his hair is always uncut and he's wearing schlubby clothes. He saved every penny, though, ended up with lots of money, and really became the most famous male porno actor. Well, he could act, you know, and he worked harder than anybody. Really. And he had a big schlong! So that helped.

He used to fall asleep while directing! In front of the monitor! Totally sober! He never did drugs in his life. Never even boozed. This guy didn't get high at any time. He was just high on himself, man. Ron Jeremy, the famous porn star with the big cock. The girls loved him, and he thought, one day, he would crossover into the mainstream. Onto Main Street. And he really became known, you know, on one of those celebrity reality TV shows. "The Surreal Life." The same season with Vanilla Ice, that white rapper who had one big hit. I can't remember anybody else in that house. So Ron like really stood out, you know what I mean? From then on, everyone knew him. All over the place, people everywhere would mention his name. And start laughing.

*

How did I get from there to here? And I'm totally straight! Usually, if I smoke a joint and start talking, then I'll be in like 30 different places in one minute, you know what I mean? There's a reason why I went here, though. If I just go back... video! Right! That's what I wanted to say. In the early '80s, the business went from film to video. And that's when everyone left San Francisco and New York and moved to Los Angeles. The plastic place! That's what I call it. We went from the gritty reality and philosophical nature of New York and San Francisco, talking about freedom and the liberation of sex, you know, to the fake plastic society of Los Angeles. Where everyone only cared about how pretty the girls were. And I must say, at that time, the models *did* get a lot prettier. California girls. Bimbos. Some of them weren't, you know, but mostly they were not too bright.

Although when I moved out to L.A., I would always look for the smartest X-rated girls to date. Me and my friend, Mark Spiegler. He was my production manager for a little while and then he became an agent. In fact, he runs one of the biggest talent agencies in the whole business: Spiegler Girls. You can look it up. Well, we would call each other up if we found smart women. He's not the best looking guy in the world. Smart though. *Really smart!* And he has tons of money, but doesn't live like it. He lives in a small apartment, drives a used Mercedes, and dresses really casually. In California, you can dress like that. No one cares. Why did I bring him up? I don't remember. Oh... intelligent girls! I was always looking for intelligent *women*. Women who could express themselves through more than just doing sex.

A lot of my best friends are these kinds of expressive women. To be honest, in my whole career, I never became good friends with many other porno actors. The men. To me, there's something obnoxious about them in general. Egotistical. Narcissistic. All my male friends have been people on the sets, cameramen, directors. On the other hand, I've had a number of friends and girlfriends who were actresses. When I would meet porno girls, if they were smart, then I would try to bring that out of them. Help them find out who they really were. And I was good at it. I guess, I never really succeeded *completely*. You can only do so much. It just depends on how much trauma or abuse happened when they were young. And if a girl really did have issues, then I would sometimes worry about putting her on camera. But if they were really popular, you know, if they were making good money, getting famous, and starting to get their self-esteem, then I wouldn't stop them, you know what I mean?

Sometimes, you might think that putting someone in an objectifying situation, like having sex on camera, is not a good idea. In my mind, though, I was *subjecting* them. Trying to bring out the good in them. By doing great sex! Being free. Not being scared. Not being repressed. And porno actresses, the X-rated stars, are less repressed than anyone when it comes to sex. That's for sure! Later, though, after so many years, most of them will quit. It can be a hard life, you know, and not everyone should do it. I definitely don't think females under 20 years old should do it. But they can start being in the movies at 18 years old, and nowadays, they start having sex at 14. In my day, that didn't happen! In fact, if a girl had sex at like 17, then she was "the town whore." Meanwhile, if a guy was able to fuck ten girls, then he was some big hero. I've always found that attitude to be totally disgusting!

But men can be prostitutes, too. John Holmes, one of the most known male actors, he was a hustler. He would prostitute for women and he'd prostitute for men. Because his dick was so giant, basically, people would pay to suck his dick. Johnny Wad. The film *Boogie Nights*, you know, is sort of based on the story of John Holmes. That was directed by Paul Thomas Anderson. He's a pretty good director, and I think that was his first movie. His first big movie, anyway. And *Boogie Nights* was about L.A. productions which there were very few at the time. There were hardly any porn movies being made in L.A. when John Holmes was making them. And his movies, you know, were typical L.A. movies. Plastic. Shitty! Even still, back in those days, everyone knew John Holmes. Even the straight people! *Oh yeah, the guy that makes the X-rated movies.*

Him and Harry Reems. Because Harry Reems was the actor from *Deep Throat* that the government took from New York, brought to Tennessee, and tried to put on trial. And Hugh Heffner actually let him hideout in the Playboy Mansion for like two years. Got him lawyers. The whole bit. But that ruined the guy's life. Harry Reems came back to the business eventually, but was a druggie and an alcoholic. Ended up moving to Utah and becoming like a Mormon salesman or something. I think he passed away a couple of years ago. I'm telling you, though, *Deep Throat* was such a phenomenon. They would double bill it with *The Devil in Miss Jones*. Those were like art movies. Well, *Deep Throat* was really just a lousy stupid movie about a girl who could deep throat. But *The Devil in Miss Jones*, the one after, with Georgina Spelvin, that was a really good picture!

There were some high art erotic movies, too. In the '70s, in New York City, I was always going to the theaters to see the new American directors and these great European directors. Like Truffaut. Before he died. And Warhol made some movies about sex, you know, involving gay cowboys or transvestites. Holly Woodlawn. I remember, she was a famous transvestite from the Andy Warhol factory. And that's when John Waters came out with Divine and *Pink Flamingos* and *Polyester.* Hey, I just saw him on Bill Maher the other night. John Waters! What a strange character! The way he dresses and everything. His whole look is so weird, man. But I loved his movies. Oh yeah. I was always going to the movies. Strip shows, sports, music, and movies. I was a real pop culture guy. Big time! I loved it all. And I really wanted to be involved in it some way, you know what I mean?

Man, my back is really hurting me. I'm not wearing my brace. If I sit in one spot for too long, after a while, my back starts killing me. Like when I go on long car trips, I can't move the next day. It's been like this for years. Because I've been walking with slumped shoulders since I was a little kid. Yeah, I walk like a monkey, so my back is all messed up. It's brutal. I used to have this guy, Dr. Frank. He would come to my house every two weeks to fix me up. Dr. Frank wasn't really a doctor, you know, but worked with some celebrities, and he was the one who recommended this brace. And I actually really love wearing it! Sort of like a corset, you know what I mean? So I have a little femaleness in me. That's what I'm saying. Shit, I used to wear women's panties. Sure. I would wear female underwear one day and regular male underwear the next. That's how wacky I was!

That started when I was a junior in high school. I wasn't getting laid or anything, so this was exciting! I just went to the fucking Woolworth's and bought them. That's all. I don't know. It made me feel good. They're much more comfortable. Men used to have to wear these tight little things. I did not like those tighty-whities! It's probably been like 20 years, you know, but I wore women's things throughout the '70s and '80s. But then, these shorts came out for men, the long-hanging basketball shorts, and now that's what I wear. I stopped with the panties a long time ago.

*

Game 1 of the NBA Finals is tonight. Who do I like? Are you kidding? The Warriors! I mean, Cleveland might put up a fight. They do have LeBron James. And their whole team has been playing well, but they're not really that good. And the Warriors have a deep team, you know, and Steph Curry. The MVP!

I was listening to Jalen Rose's podcast on *Grantland*. And he said the only two players in NBA history who remind him of Steph Curry, you know, quick little guards who were both tremendous shooters and really great passers, are Bob Cousy and Tiny Archibald. And he didn't say Isiah Thomas! I'm thinking, I bet he gets tons of emails and – what do you call them? – tweets, you know, asking, "What about Isiah? What about Isiah?" Seriously. Are you old enough to remember how great Isiah Thomas was? There was one playoff game where he got 29 points in one quarter. On a broken leg! He was a terrible coach though. One of the worst of all time! Ran the Knicks right into the ground. Well, I don't entirely blame him. James Dolan's the owner of the Knicks, you know, and he's a total disaster! I have no idea why Phil Jackson took that coaching job. I guess, he was pissed at Jerry Buss. Phil went to his house, and Buss said, "I'm gonna hire you." And then, the next night, he hired Mike D'Antoni. Big mistake! He's a terrible coach!

Okay. D'Antoni had his system in Phoenix, and with the right players, it can work. And they did get screwed a couple of years ago. Do you remember, in Game 5 of some playoff series, during a scrum, Amar'e Stoudemire came off the bench for like a second. So he was suspended for the next game, and Phoenix lost the series. He didn't do anything! He took one little footstep onto the court. And Larry O'Brien suspended him. In the playoffs! Game 6! You can't do that. I mean, *David Stern* suspended him. What did I say? Larry O'Brien? Who's Larry O'Brien?

CHAPTER 5
SOCIAL STUDIES

Lately, I've really been watching a lot of American Hero. I told you about this new station that came on like a month ago. It's so tremendous.

Who turned me on to it? Bruce/Will Divide! I was staying at his house near Thousand Oaks. He has cancer, you know, so I was helping him out. He first got it in his thumb and had to have it amputated. Three years later, the cancer moved to another area. Anyway, one day, I was at Bruce/Will Divide's house, and he was watching all this war stuff. I said, "What is this shit?" He said, "It's this great new station. I've never seen this footage before." And he was right! There's tons of different footage from every American war. Even from the Revolutionary War, you know, they reenacted the whole thing. Did you know that Washington wasn't really the first general? It was some doctor from Boston, but he got killed in battle. And then Washington took over, and they started marching south. The Revolutionary War started up north, you know, and that's when the French saved our ass. If it wasn't for the French, there would never even have been a revolution.

That's why when we saved France, in like WWI, our soldiers went to the grave of Lafayette. He was the French patriot that helped the Americans get their independence. The French, you know, were the first people to have their revolution. And it's only been in like the last 20 years, all of a sudden, that Americans don't like the French anymore. Frogs and Freedom Fries. Da da da. Before that, we loved everything to do with the French. Poets and writers. Jazz musicians. Everyone went to Paris. And the French invented sex. French kissing. Oral sex. I love the French! And they have great food, man. I mean, I get sick from their food, but it's great! Just too rich for my system. When I lived in New York City, my wife Stacy and I would go to fancy French restaurants, but I haven't had any in years. Shit. It costs a fortune.

On American Hero, of course, they're always showing things about WWII. The beginning of the American Empire! Before then, you know, we didn't care about going to other parts of the world and getting into everyone's business. We were always isolationist. Except for Teddy Roosevelt during the Spanish-American War. That was like 1890-something and only lasted for six months. That's how we ended up with Puerto Rico, I think, and the Philippines. But once we became the big shot, we turned into a military aggressor, you know, and have been at war for basically 70 years straight! After WWII, the Cold War started, and it was like we were at war with Russia. I remember being on a bus, 12 years old, and hearing how there were Russian nuclear warheads in Cuba pointed right at us. We might all be annihilated.

And, remember, in the early '50s, we had McCarthy going around accusing everyone of being a communist. Anyone who was Jewish, or an artist, or an intellectual, you know, he'd put them on his blacklist. This guy was out of control! He was a fascist! Like Mussolini. He fucking went after everyone, until it finally came out that he was lying about everything. Edward R. Murrow, one of my all-time favorite journalists, was the one who broke the story. At least, then, you know, the news reporters were all *sort of* objective. That's why Walter Cronkite could have run for president and won. He was on television every night, telling the truth. In 1968, Cronkite came out and said that he didn't think we should be in Vietnam, and that gave a lot of steam to the anti-war people, man. We weren't just freaks and hippies and college kids anymore.

Though, most of the time, the press portrayed hippies as just people doing drugs and fucking and not caring about work or anything else in the straight world. And regular people didn't know any better. There weren't any hippies in Sharon. No Beats or hipsters or anything alternative. They say sometimes, in the '50s, behind the curtains, there was some weird stuff going on. Like wife-swapping, you know, but I never saw that. I mean, it's true that my father wasn't home a lot. He'd be at work or the gym. My friends used to say, "I bet he was with another woman." No. I really never thought my father was cheating, but I also don't know how much sex my mother would have. Probably "lights off," you know what I mean? Because the whole thing growing up was pitch black, close the shades, wait 'til the kids are asleep completely, you know, and then maybe there would be a little action.

When I was 11 years old, I remember my mother coming into my bedroom. I had cum during the night, you know, and there were some stains on my pajamas. I remember her asking me: "What's this?" I said, "I don't know, Ma. You tell me!" She never talked about stuff like that! I'm telling you, sexuality was never mentioned in my house. Ever. And there was no sex education in the schools. Not even in gym class. Nothing. Zero! I picked everything up from the so-called streets. And talking with friends. That said, almost every kid I knew was a virgin, you know, some of them never went out with anyone. We were all like little nerds. Nervous nerds. We didn't know anything! And when I started thinking about sex and jerking off, I would feel tons of guilt afterwards and be totally confused. I'd think, "What did I just do?"

And since I was a kid, for some reason, I've always been fascinated by giant breasts. I don't know why. *I do know why!* My fifth grade teacher: Mrs. Mitchell. She had giant tits and was really fucking pretty! There were a couple of boys in the class who would always cause trouble, and when they did, she would punish everyone. If it was time for recess, and no one spoke up and told on them, then she would make the whole class stay in. My fifth grade teacher made a big imprint on me, you know, on the type of woman that I like. And it was connected to punishment! Maybe that's why I got into the whole S&M thing? Female domination. That's a big era in a person's life, you know, adolescence rolling in, and I have this giant-titted, beautiful, Amazon, woman teacher, and she's punishing us. The wrong people. We didn't do anything!

The Jewish kids got the short end, once again, you know what I mean? The Jewish kids wouldn't cause any trouble! We just got the punishment. It was these two fucking townie kids who were always causing trouble. Old Sharon townies, you know, the non-Jewish kids who lived in the center of town. A lot of the Jewish kids were scared of these townies because they would always pick on us. But we shouldn't have let those townies push us around! At ten years old, we should have looked at what happened in WWII and said, "We're not going to take it anymore!"

*

I just love big tits so much! I'm like Russ Meyer. He was the first guy to show naked breasts on the big screen. They were action movies where women were the aggressors and always had *the biggest tits ever*. His original picture was called *The Immoral Mister Teas*. It was about a guy who wore these special glasses that allowed him to see through women's shirts.

One of his last movies, you know, he actually co-wrote with Roger Ebert. What was it called? I can't remember. Wait... let me just go to IMDB. Let's see... okay. Russ Meyer. Here we go... *The Immoral Mister Teas*. 1959. *Eve and the Handyman*. 1961. *Heavenly Bodies!* 1963. *Lorna*. 1964. That was huge! With Lorna Maitland. And *Fanny Hill*. And *Faster Pussycat! Kill! Kill!* I remember *Vixen!* 1968. There was this woman who played the vixen. What does that say? Erica Gavin. "Is she a woman... or an animal?" Because the women were so aggressive! Oh! Here it is. *Beyond the Valley of the Dolls*. 1970. There was a movie just called *Valley of the Dolls* based on the book, you know, but Russ Meyer's was different. Roger Ebert wrote the script with him, and they had a big budget from the studio. Mass marketed and everything. In color. The whole bit. That's the one! Thank you very much.

I based a lot of my moviemaking on his style. When I shot some movies for Big Top, you know, during the late '80s and early '90s, I cast women with breasts like *this*. In those days, the girls had just started getting their breasts done. Originally, we were basically just using fat girls. Girls with giant tits that would hang. Now, with this new plastic surgery, girls were becoming freaks. Sex freaks! And that's who we would shoot at Big Top. Because I was trying to do like Russ Meyer movies. I came up with this series called *Pussy Power*. They weren't really big features. Just little scenes, and we'd string like four scenes together and make a film. The women would come in, strip for a guy, and then just *sit on the guy's face* and smother him. That was my favorite. I love pussy, you know, so I want the pussy right on top of my face.

This is what came to be known as the "face-sitting" movie. I kind of invented it. Back then, we just called them "smother" movies, you know what I mean? I had met this guy who made wrestling movies with the artist Eric Stanton. And I shot these movies for them where women would wrestle men and always beat them with scissorholds. I didn't really want to do them, but I knew the guy, and he asked me for a favor. So I was doing one of these scissorhold movies, and I said, "How about this idea? Instead of having the girl scissorhold the guy, instead of capturing his neck with her legs and thighs, why not just have the girl sit on the guy? *Squash him*. So he can't breathe. You're doing the same thing with the legs, and I bet you'll do much better." And he did. Boom! He stopped doing those stupid scissorhold movies after that.

And then I went to Big Top myself and said, "Listen. I have an idea. No sex. It's just nakedness, tease, and it might be something unique and different that your fans will like." I must have shot like five of those *Pussy Power* movies for Big Top, you know, and shortly after, that led to *Pussyman*.

*

Tease is my thing. I love teasing. And I love to be teased. That turns me on, man. She has the power, you know, and I can't do anything about it. I remember, at the clubs, I would always sit in the front row. At first, I was scared and would hang in the back, but after a while, I went up front. The strippers would take my glasses and rub them against their pussy, or their tits, and then put them back on my nose. I thought that was tremendous! Where most people wouldn't. A lot of guys, you know, when they go into clubs and get teased, they come out and say, "But I didn't get laid!" So what? You had a great time! You'll get laid another time. What's the big deal?

I had a number of those discussions in the '70s when I would go to strip clubs with my friends. One of my friends was a vice president at CitiBank. That's how I ended up in this giant house on Atlantic Beach, next to Long Beach, you know, in this really rich area of Long Island. We had a private beach and everything! Lisa and I moved there with my really good friend Lenny, remember, who had returned from Vietnam. And then there was this vice president of CitiBank and his girlfriend, a little dancer named Pepe. We'd all walk down the street, the girls in their little bikinis, and everyone would just stare at us. This was a pretty conservative area, you know, and we weren't really supposed to be living there. We were in the wrong place, man. We just got the house because of my friend, this bank vice president.

I originally met Lisa in Ithaca, New York, coming back from one of my hitchhiking trips. Right before I left for the trip, I started dating – remember I told you about my big-titted college friend, Andrea? – her younger sister Valerie. She was the same age as my sister, Bonnie. So I went cross-country, you know, and on the way back to New York City, I stopped at Ithaca College for almost two months. Valerie was living there, and her roommate was... Lisa! I'll never forget. I watched the George Foreman-Muhammad Ali fight in the Ithaca Student Center. "The Rumble in the Jungle." Ithaca was a beautiful place, but when it started getting cold, you know, it was time for me to go back to the city. So, yeah, Lisa liked me from the beginning, you know what I mean? And then Valerie and I broke up like six months later.

That summer, when I moved to Long Beach with my friend, Lisa called me up one day and said, "Hey, listen, I'm going to be around the beach. Can I come down to your house?" I didn't know she was after me. I just thought she was my friend from being up in Ithaca, but she was *after me*. And we were friends, you know, so sometimes we had sex. That's the way it was in those days. Easy. No big deal. Eventually, though, she was like, "Can I stay here for a while?" And that's when she got me. That was 1975 when we first got together. And she also became incredibly close with my sister. When we went to Boston, I took her to meet my family, and Lisa and Bonnie got along immediately. *Fast friends!* They told each other everything. So that part of her I really liked, you know what I mean?

When Lisa and I first lived together, she was waitressing around the city. I was like, "Fuck this waitress stuff. You could make more money dancing in the clubs." So she listened to me and did it. Yeah, for like six months, she danced in one of those brand new clubs they started building in the '70s. This place in Manhattan. City Corps. It was a *beautiful* location. With *beautiful* lights and *beautiful* women. It was the nicest, classiest club in New York. She didn't mind it, you know, especially once she started making the money. She'd probably say now that she hated it? I don't know. But, at the time, she was like, "Wow! Look how much money I made tonight!" When I was working for my father, I'd come back to the city on Thursday night and pick her up at the club. Maybe stay for a while and watch with everyone else. I didn't care. She wasn't doing anything. She was just dancing nude. I'd even throw the dollars at her. Boom! Boom! Boom!

*

For a time, in the late '70s, I didn't do any movies. But some of those years are a little confusing, you know, I don't remember exactly what or when I did anything. Because I did a lot of different little things, man. That whole time with Lisa, you know, I wasn't fully in the business. I was either working for her dad, or my dad, or at that record store, Disco-Mat. Somewhere in there, I got my master's in Education from Long Island University and a certificate to teach in New York State for life. No kidding. Grades 7-12. I even taught some high school History on Long Island, you know, subbed for a while in Long Beach and Lawrence and all over the five boroughs. And when I was teaching, I wasn't doing movies. No, but I was always on the fringes. *Connected*. As soon as the school year would end, and summer began, I was still in touch with some people.

One year, I actually had a regular full-time teaching gig. Glen Cove High on Long Island. Social Studies. I tried to teach the students everything I knew, you know, help them get away from the traditional ideas. I wanted them to feel good about themselves. Most of the other teachers, they didn't care about the kids, man, so that really turned me off. In the teachers' lounge, the only thing they talked about was tenure. I don't really remember that many particular students, but I did try to help this one girl. I wasn't supposed to, I guess, but her home life was so fucked up. Hey, I didn't do anything with her! I had my – what do you call it? – morals. You probably think, "Oh, he went after her! How could they let him be a teacher? He did porno!" So what? I just tried to give her confidence. Teach her about the right things. Or, at least, what I thought were the right things to teach.

That's why I quit. I was so idealistic, and none of the other teachers really cared. So I said, "Fuck this!" I won't be part of a system that continually tries to control and manipulate kids. Everything I did, you know, I wanted to do alternative stuff from the norm. Because the norms were all crooks. And too structured! Much too structured for me, man! I remember, when I graduated in 1972, my friend and I had this big discussion. After graduation, now that we'd learned that most of what we were taught in high school was bullshit – that it was society's way of controlling us and putting us into these little slots – were we going to go back to the old way of life? Or continue to live for the freedom of everyone? We asked each other: "What's it going to be?" And I said to myself, "I'm not going back. This is who I am now."

But a lot of people did go back to their old towns, you know, and back to being who they were before they changed their lives. Not me. I believed in freedom and I hated structure. That's why the alternative lifestyle, you know, for me, it was tremendous.

*

I always say, "tremendous." That's my word! I like those kinds of words, you know, "spectacular," "amazing." Grandiose words. To make a point. At times, I like to exaggerate. I used to *really* exaggerate *all of the time*. I would describe everything to my friends like I was a sports announcer. That's just how I would speak. I mean, I'm not doing that here – no! – but I do have a tendency to exaggerate.

I can't remember where I picked up "tremendous." Mike Graffone uses the word "tremendous," too. I don't know if he picked it up from me, or me from him, but he said he got it from Boston. I don't know. I've just been saying it forever. I actually have a hat that Bruce/Will Divide made for me that says: TREMENDOUS. I wear it everywhere! And when I write something, and it's really good, I'll put it in capital letters: TREMENDOUS. And you know what I really hate? In texts and emails, I like to put things in capital letters. And the first time I wrote someone an email in capital letters, they wrote back, "You piece of shit!" If it's in capital letters, I guess, then you're like yelling at the other person. Why? That's the stupidest thing I've ever heard! I'm not yelling at you. I'm old! I'm making it easier for you to see.

Really, though, I don't know what's happening on the computer half the time. I know how to work like 30% of the computer and only 20% of my phone. I told you, my whole life, I've had this battle against machines! And they are eventually going to totally fuck us over. Oh yeah. Somewhere along the line, we'll make the machines so powerful, and humans are so violent and greedy, that the machines will somehow… who knows? We're almost there already. Because we are too stupid and rely so much on machines. "Give it to the machine! Give it to the machine!" The machine, the machine, the machine, the machine. And they'll pick up human emotions, you know, and a lot of human emotions these days are fear and jealousy and stuff like that. Why won't the machines pick that up?

But with all the pollution and climate change, who knows what could happen? Natural disasters. And the terrorists nowadays! I'm always a little worried about terrorists. Back when we were bombed in 2001, I said to my friends, we should like get gas masks and arm ourselves, just in case. I'm against guns, sure, but I think that if no one else had them, you know, only the government and the police, then that could lead to heavy fascist control. Like during the Boston Marathon a few years ago, when they caught that kid in Watertown, and they showed the Watertown cops. I thought it was some country's militia! *It was the cops!* They have so many weapons now. I usually hate gun people, don't get me wrong, but I think that we could easily end up as a fascist society. Where the corporations are in charge and have all of the weapons. And then it's over. That's the end.

The other night, I was watching an episode of *Vice* on the "The New Cold War." This was a very enlightening episode. They interviewed Obama and Biden and a few Russian heads. Not the main dude, Putin, but the head of the army and some other advisors. And they all said, "Things are not looking good. NATO is right on our borders. It's like the Cuban missile crisis in reverse." Those little countries, you know, that were behind the Iron Curtain, well, now they're all with NATO. Latvia and Lithuania and Ukraine. When the Wall came down, and they went back to being independent, who did they go to for help? That's right. The United States! So we have tons of military bases and troops in those places. We have missiles along the Russian border! And Russia, they've lined up their planes and their tanks and their submarines. If anything happens, you know, one stupid fucking thing sets it off, and everyone could just nuke each other. There's your apocalypse.

Or maybe diseases will knock everyone out? It easily could happen. And governments make up their own diseases. I'm a big conspiracy person, of course, but I think AIDS was designed by the U.S. government. To get rid of gay people, black people, heroin addicts. Think about it. Here in the United States, in the '70s, everybody was rising up. The Black Panthers. The Gay Rights movement. This and that. Russia, you know, was known for years to get rid of half their population. The Cossacks would kill the peasants because there were too many people and not enough food. And that's another big thing! We have too many people living in the world now. People live longer and longer and longer and they don't stop with the babies. I don't want to get into how many kids people should have, but – c'mon! – eight, nine, ten kids. God! Have 20 kids, and they give you a television show.

I don't have any kids. I've had two abortions. Well, not me personally. One of them was around the year 2000. That's when I wanted a kid *badly*. I had had a dream when I was like 25 years old that when I was like 40-something, you know, I would meet this woman about 30, and we'd have a kid. It was like a premonition and – boom! – there it was. The dream I had in my 20s was coming true. I remember coming back from Boston, taking some of that Viagra shit, and I hadn't seen… Tracy… I always get Stacy and Tracy mixed up… I hadn't seen *Tracy* for like a whole month. I had been in Boston after my father passed away. So I came back to L.A., took a Viagra, and I just knew that I got her pregnant. Because I came deep inside her. Sure enough, she got pregnant. But it didn't work out. My father died. Her father was sick. And then Tracy got really depressed, and everything went to shit.

II

CHAPTER 6
MORE, MORE, MORE

How do you want to start? What year are we in? Do you want to ask me a question or should we just roll? So my very first movie was Gerard Damiano's *Portrait*, and I was only in that one scene. Truthfully, I don't really remember what the movie was about, probably a portrait of Jody Maxwell coming to New York City. I don't know. I have no idea. In those days, when I was in a movie, I didn't care what it was about! I was only in one scene, so shit. What did I care?

There were two kinds of shoots. The "one-day wonders," where they would shoot a whole movie in the middle of the night. I was in a bunch of those movies because you didn't have to be a good actor. In New York, we shot in warehouses, lofts, and a few houses. For the bigger features, the two-three week shoots, they would set up in these mansions. I remember being on set at the Woolworth, this estate on Long Island. These were huge crews, like regular film crews, you know what I mean? Then there would be a long script and a whole big story. I had roles in a number of Chuck Vincent pictures. He was a huge director who made some bigger budget movies. I was also in some movies by Henri Pachard. Well, his real name was Ron Sullivan. In the late '60s, he had produced a classic cult hit called *Putney Swope*. Somewhere in the '70s, though, Ron Sullivan became Henri Pachard, this famous director of porn.

I didn't have any humongous roles, but was in a lot of little movies and also had minor roles in some big movies. I would always get cast as a hippie. I had the right look, the right clothes, you know, overalls and jumpsuits. These crazy-colored one-piece things. And I had no stomach then.

I was thin as you could possibly be. Skinny as shit. Everyone thought I was Puerto Rican, maybe with a bit of Italian. I always had hair like *this*, you know, and didn't even have to fro it. It was just like that. Fucking long and curly. Big hair and a big black mustache. Of course, there was a difference between being a hippie and playing a hippie. And the word "hippie" meant different things to different people. The real hippies lived on communes, completely outside of society. People like me, we weren't *true* hippies. We just called ourselves hippies, you know, because we had long hair, smoked pot, and lived a totally alternative lifestyle.

There were actually some occasions when I wouldn't get a role because I refused to cut my hair. But when I started making the "loops," they didn't care. The loops were just these one-scene movies shot on 8mm. For instance, I'd be a bellboy, and there would be a woman in a hotel room. She'd invite me in for a drink, and the next thing you know, we'd start having sex. That was it. The loops were great. For me? Perfect! I didn't have to memorize 50,000 lines. I never went to acting school. I wasn't a *natural* actor, and in these loops, you could just be yourself. For the most part, they were just standard sex scenes. Blowjob. Eating. Fucking. Three positions: ten minutes in one position, ten minutes in another position, ten minutes in another position. Done. There was a couple who shot them, a man and a woman. I can't remember their names, but they never became famous, and they didn't do any heavy directing. If the sex was good, they just let you go.

Also, right after that first movie, I got an agent. Dorothy Palmer. That's where I met Ron Jeremy. In her office! The rest was all word-of-mouth. My friend Michael, you know, who got me into the business, he became a lighting guy and was always on a crew. He would let me know if there was anything going on. For a loop, you'd be there for an hour. I would do two a day and get $75 a loop. That's a $150 a day. Do that twice a week and make $300. That's pretty good! On the bigger sets, you got paid by the day, but you never knew if your turn would definitely come. It was scheduled, but you could be there all day, get paid, and not even do a scene. And, many times, on these sets, people would fool around while they were waiting. It was the era of free love, man, and people really *liked* sex! Sometimes, by the time their scene came, they couldn't do it! They'd been hanging around and hanging around, you know, and finally, 8:00 at night, when they got the call, it was like, "I already had sex twice today!"

In those days, for the most part, there wasn't a large flow of talent. That's what they call performers – "talent" – and there wasn't a large flow. Especially guys. Because most guys couldn't do it. It's not easy! Back then, there was no Viagra. There was no nothing, you know what I mean? I would be a little anxious right before the scene, sure, because I knew that I had to do that "pop shot" or else. Some people say there were "fluffers," you know, women who would get the male performers ready. Bunch of bullshit. Once in a great while, on a big, big shoot, they might hire someone to hang around for the day just in case. But that's been totally overdone! No, at first, I would just have a shot of tequila. Until tequila became poison to me, and I couldn't even get it up. Of course, I always smoked a joint before every scene. That was key. Always. Forever. Right up to the present! Although I never needed too much assistance. I'm an exhibitionist and a voyeur both, you know, so I was perfect for this business!

I've always been an exhibitionist. I was an exhibitionist back when I lived in Sharon. I would like… I've never told anyone this. When I was like 15 years old, I was really attracted to my mother's friend, our next door neighbor. I wanted her. And I thought she liked me, too. I know! How could she like me? Anyway, I remember, there was no one else home, and I was down in the garage and got horny. She had an upstairs window that looked right down upon our yard. So I went outside, you know, *with a hard-on*, hoping that she would see me. I just kept staring up at her window, hoping and hoping. I must have done that two or three times. It never worked! So that was kind of me being an exhibitionist at an early age. You know what I mean? Big time!

*

I guess you could say that I found my element. For one thing, I didn't have to pick up women, you know, go to a bar, make a whole bunch of advances, and then go on five or ten dates or whatever. I mean, back in those days, you would only have to go out a few times. This was the swinging '70s in New York! Did I have a girlfriend? I usually had girlfriends, yeah, but they never cared that I did porno.

I did have one girlfriend who was an actress. Helen Madigan was her name. She'd been in the business for a while already, and I met her doing a loop. She was a hot, slutty, Irish chick with huge tits! So we were going out for a stretch, and I said, "Let's go visit my parents." My friend Lenny wanted to come along too, you know, so we made it a whole road trip. When we got to my parents house, Helen walked in with her shirt like down to here. And we were pretty high already, but then we got smashed. We stayed there for a few days and did Quaaludes the entire time! After I got back to New York, I called up The Mars and asked, "What did you think of Helen?" The Mars said, "Never bring her back here again! She's a real slutty girl!" My dad loved her, though, you know what I mean? He liked all the women that I brought home!

That didn't last too long with Helen, and right after, I started going out with Lisa. And then, eventually, Lisa and I, we got married. And how we got married… that's a great story. The five of us living at this big house on Atlantic Beach. I told you, me, Lisa, Lenny, the vice president of CitiBank, and Pepe, we're all hanging around, high on something. All of a sudden, Lenny goes, "Hey, why don't you guys get married?" I'd been with Lisa for like a year and half now. I go, "What? I'm against marriage, man! Marriage is like the traditional way of being." And then Lisa goes, "Well, my father has been saving money for a huge wedding. If we get married, maybe people will give us some money. We can go on a vacation, down to the islands or wherever." So I go, "Okay. Yeah, let's get married!" And they all went, "Yeah! Yeah! Get married! Get married! It'll be a big event."

And that's what it became: a big event. We had this huge wedding on some golf course in New Jersey. Yeah, it was like a giant fucking golf course wedding. Really extravagant. The whole bit. My friend Lenny was the best man, you know, but he definitely did not dress like you are supposed to for a wedding. He wore shoes with no socks and didn't have the typical tuxedo. I think that I wore a tux for the wedding. I mean, I wasn't wearing one of my crazy jumpsuits, but I was really high. I wasn't straight, I'll tell you that! And we had a great time! We had a tremendous party, got a ton of money, and then went to Paradise Island for ten days. When we got back to the city, we finally left the beach and moved into a place with her brother. He was an environmentalist, and a deejay, and a graffiti artist, and we lived with him for a while. Our apartment was in SoHo, right down the street from CBGB.

*

That was the summer of '77. The other day, you know, I just happened to be flipping channels and came across an old Spike Lee movie, *Summer of Sam*. I hadn't seen that movie in a long time, but it brought back a ton of memories. That was the summer that I got married. And so many other things happened! First of all, there was a tremendous heat wave. It was probably the hottest summer in 50 years. Over 100 degrees, every day, for the entire summer! Plus, in the city, if it's over 100 degrees for more than a week, with the heat and humidity mixed together, then it starts to really smell.

In July, the murders started. Some killer was going around shooting couples in parked cars. They'd be on a date or whatever, making out, and this guy would shoot them both. He was killing couples, left and right, man, and the city was in a panic. Everyone in New York was petrified to go anywhere at night. And then, in the middle of July, while these murders are taking place, during this humongous heat wave – guess what happens? – the whole city goes into a blackout! And this blackout doesn't just last for a half hour. Or an hour. Or even an hour and a half! Or two hours! It happened at night, you know, and lasted for almost the entire next day. People didn't know what was going on and started going crazy! There was looting, and fires, and complete blackout, and such miserable heat, and the murders continued on.

This is also when the punk movement had just began, and these guys in the Spike Lee movie, you know, Italians from the neighborhood, they are searching for their friend who had become this big punk. But they don't know anything about punks! They have absolutely no idea. So they *freak* out and think, because he's now a punk, that he might actually be this murderer. They are out to find him and beat the fuck out of him! They're not even going to call the cops. And then, they end up at CBGB, right around where I moved a few months later, and see all these punk people hanging outside, you know, with their spiked hairdos and leather collars. And they go inside and see the punks moshing. Slamming into each other. Falling on the floor. You know how it was with those original punks. I don't have to tell you. It was a wild scene!

Me? I was always looking for rebellious music of any kind, so sure, I gave punk a try right off the bat. I liked more of the artistic, intellectual, punk groups, you know, like Talking Heads. I wasn't really into that: "Ba ba ba. Ba ba ba. I'm rebelling! I'm rebelling! I'm rebelling! I'm rebelling!" Do you know the Ramones? The Ramones are real punk, okay, and I like the Ramones, *but I don't*. I need a hook somewhere, you know, some catchy words or something. Like Blondie. Debbie Harry. I had every one of her albums. And Patti Smith. I loved Patti Smith! Between her great words, amazing vocals, and being an aggressive, sexual, female lead, she is one of my all-time favorites. Back in those days, in New York, I actually saw her on the street a few times, and she sort of looked like Keith Richards. But she looked good! Tough. Leather. My kind of look! And she was a poet. She was just like: "Fuck the rules! Yeah! Fuck you! This is me!"

When I think about it, there wasn't a lot of punk in the adult film world. Not like nowadays where, I told you, half the women who do porno movies are fully illustrated. At this time, though, there was no influence of punk. Disco was the thing because disco led immediately to sex. In the late '70s, New York was just like one giant dance party. As a matter of the fact, there was a big porno star who had a #1 song. Andrea True Connection. That was the name of the group. Andrea True was her name, and the song was called "More, More, More." I remember Helen Madigan playing it for me in our apartment. She said, "My friend, an actress who you've never worked with, made this record. She met some sugar daddy, and he produced it for her." And the next thing you know, it was #1 in the disco clubs. And the next thing you know, it crossed over into the top 40. I'm watching Billboard every week, and it's rising and rising and rising.

Finally, it went all the way to #1. On the regular charts! "More, More, More." You could probably find it on YouTube, you know what I mean? It went to the top of the pop charts! So I thought that was pretty amazing. And, in those days, all of a sudden, there were these tremendous new disco singers that no one had ever heard of before. Gloria Gaynor was one of the biggest, you know, "I Will Survive." Giorgio Moroder was the #1 producer and did tremendous work on the synthesizers. He might have even done "More, More, More"? I don't know. But he was the one who produced for Donna Summer. I love, love, love Donna Summer. Oh yeah! Donna Summer was one of the original, aggressive, female singers, and she had so many sexy songs. "Bad Girls" and "Hot Stuff" and "Love to Love You Baby." Yes! Donna Summer. Donna Summer of Sam!

They finally caught that guy, you know, David Berkowitz, on the last day of July. He had like too many outstanding parking tickets or something, and they tracked him down. It turned out, there was this dog, a Labrador named Sam, who lived across the street and would always somehow end up at his door. When Sam barked, Berkowitz thought the dog was telling him to go murder people. That's why he's called the Son of Sam. He heard that dog say, "Go right now and kill some good-looking girls!" So he said, "Okay, I will. You're the devil. I'll do whatever you say." At least, that's how they showed it in the movie. But, you know, I remember, that's basically kind of what happened.

*

I knew that marriage wasn't going to last forever. In fact, it didn't really even last that long. It started in 1977 on a Caribbean honeymoon, and by the next year, my father had called me back to Boston to work at State Beef. So I was only seeing Lisa on the weekends. She was getting her master's at NYU, and I found out that, while I was away, she was going with someone from college, you know, fucking cheating on me!

Well, basically, you could say, a regular civilian, you know, that person could say that I was cheating, too. By doing porno movies. But they didn't mean anything to me. It was a job. That's the way we looked at it back then. I still do. I mean, yeah, it's a very enjoyable job. And I've always said, you know, you should try to find a job doing something that you really love. Don't do something that's going to make you miserable for your whole life. It doesn't matter how much money you make! To me, money was never the important thing. Sure, I wanted it. I knew it was important to have. But I never cared about being like a millionaire. And Lisa, and all my friends, they knew that I was in movies and thought it was cool. They all sort of thought of me as like a celebrity, you know what I mean? And I never got involved with any of the porno girls. At least, not back then.

I certainly had my favorites though. Yeah, I remember a few. My favorite actress, her name was Veri Knotty. She looked like Grace Slick and was the first woman in the business to wear like the thigh-high boots. She also wore leather at times, you know, and those tough outfits turn me on! Veri Knotty.

There were two reasons for her name. First of all, she was a wild performer, so that's why she called herself "naughty." Plus, she had the biggest pussy lips I've ever seen in my life and – get this! – she would tie them in a knot. Thus... the name "Knotty." Double entendre. Two meanings. Because they were so long, you know, she could tie her lips in a knot, and that was all part of her thing. She was a freak, man, and everyone loved it! And she was good-looking, too, and one of my very favorites from that era.

There wasn't anything that I was particularly known for as a performer, but I always liked to eat pussy. In those days, I remember, there was so much hair. Women would grow their hair like heavy jungle. Almost down to the knees! I used to make a joke that I would have to like take a rake and rake through the hair to even see the pussy, you know what I mean? Eventually, they began to realize that these were X-rated movies, man, and the audience actually wants to see the vagina. They just don't want to see bush. So the girls started shaving a little. By the mid '80s, you know, they were shaving everything off. Somewhere in the late '70s, when I first *really* saw a girl's genitals, you know, she had shaved so you could really see her pussy, I went bananas! I was like, "Wow! Shaved pussy! I can see everything! This is what I'm looking for!"

Cunnilingus was my favorite thing. Of course! Most guys, you know, they never cared about going down on women. Some guys would even refuse to do it. They didn't care about the pleasure of the woman. I always cared about the pleasure of the woman! When I was young, I said to myself, "Wow! If I can be good at this, you know, become an expert, then I'll have no trouble. I'll get huge points." And I did. *I got huge points!* Because I was really good at it. Superb. I did it so often, and the porno scenes were a really good place to practice. Everyone knew why we were there and what we were supposed to do. I told you, it wasn't like I had to go to a bar, pick a woman up, and go through that whole routine, you know, before I could finally get down to the vagina and go to work!

Oh god. I'm trying to remember a few more of the actresses from that time. There were just so many women. One of my first movies was with Teri Hall. She was a big star for a while. There was Samantha Fox. I remember her. And, of course, Vanessa del Rio. She was a pretty Cuban with giant tits and a huge clitoris. And she was wild sexually. The women, these actresses, got really big because their names were always on the marquees. Like Seka. She was a big female porno star in the late '70s, early '80s, and her name was always up there. And Marilyn Chambers. *Behind the Green Door*. Everyone wanted to see that movie once they found that she was the Ivory Snow girl. Once in a while, they would put a guy's name on the marquee, you know, like John Holmes or Harry Reems, but not very often.

In the loops, you never knew any of the guys. You didn't know anyone! When you bought a loop, it never said who was in the film. And to see a loop, you'd have to go into one of the bookstores. Once you were there, you could either buy a loop and take it home or stay and watch it on the little machine. You'd walk into a booth, you know, sit down on a little seat, put your quarter in the machine, and the movie would come on. If you wanted to watch a loop at home, then you had to buy a projector and play it off the wall. So I bought my own projector and would screen my movies wherever I was living. When I was getting my master's, living in Great Neck by myself in a basement apartment, I remember projecting against the wall. Yeah, I loved seeing myself. I always have. I don't know what you call that or anything, but it's always been an extra turn on.

Especially on the big screen! That was tremendous. I mean, there was *my cock*, and it would look 900 ft. long. Instead of, you know, whatever it actually is. In the porno business, of course, they always look for big dicks. Mine is like medium to big. It's good. It's fine. A lot of the girls don't want these giant things in them. Are you kidding? C'mon!

*

When I was a kid, you know, ten years old, I really wanted to be a weatherman. It started, I think, when I saw that weathermen never got into trouble. Their predictions were always wrong, and yet, they never got fired from their jobs, or yelled at, or anything. I remember asking my father: "Dad, what's with this? Everyone else, if they do something wrong, they get punished. But weathermen are wrong all the time. Constantly! And they just laugh, make jokes with each other. This and that. It's like the greatest job in history." He had no answer. What kind of answer could he have? That's just the way it goes for weathermen.

So my parents bought me a barometer, a weather vane, all kinds of weather equipment. Seriously. That's how much I was into it. And since then, I've always been into the weather. I remember, Bonnie had cable TV before I did, and when I would visit her, all I would do is watch MTV and the Weather Channel. I loved the Weather Channel! I don't watch it much anymore, but I still check the weather every day. For Encino, you know, I'll look at like ten different websites. I always know what the weather is going to be. At least, what *they* say it's going to be. My mother was the same way. The Mars, anyone she talked to, from anywhere, the first thing that she would ask: "What's the weather?" If I was in another city: "What's the weather? What's the weather?" So that's probably where I picked it up. Being a weatherman, you know, that would have been a good gig for me. And I'm still interested in it. Quite a bit. I haven't changed.

But that's not the gig that I ended up with. No, I didn't become a weatherman! Or a meatman or a teacher or a lamp salesman. Like I said, I went back to State Beef for like seven months, one final time. And then, for a while, when I came back to New York, I substituted a little and did the light fixture job. But then it was basically over for me in the straight world. There was nowhere to sub, and I tried to get a regular teaching job, but couldn't. That's when I was walking around Manhattan, working for my father-in-law, you know, getting more and more pissed because he promised me this whole huge empire and didn't come through. After that, Lisa and I broke up, and I went back into the sex business for good. I needed to make a paycheck. Plus, I really *wanted* to get back into it, you know, so I jumped in all the way.

I don't really remember many of those features from the late '70s. I think maybe there was a big picture called *Takeoff* from 1978. I don't remember what it was about. Sex on an airplane? I could find out. I mean, I just have to go to IMDB and look up David Christopher. Or Pussyman. Hey, maybe I'll do that right now! Should I? Okay. David... Christopher... Here we go. *Night of Submission*. 1976. Like a one-day quasi-S&M picture. I don't really remember much about it. I just remember the name. *Untamed Vixens*. 1976. I've never even heard of it! *She's No Angel*. 1976. Don't remember it at all. *Sharon*. 1977. Sharon! Really? No recollection. That might be a mistake. I'm listed all the time, you know, but I don't think I was in that picture. As a matter of fact, many times, they would change the title of the movie. Yeah, nine times out of ten, by the time they finally put a movie out, it was called something totally different.

Okay. A few more. *French Teen*. 1977. I remember that one. Stupid, ridiculous, goofy, little movie. *Heat Wave*. 1977. Hey, I told you about the big heat wave in 1977. Maybe it was about that summer in New York? Maybe I played a weatherman? That would be tremendous! No, to tell you the truth, I don't remember ever playing a weatherman. And – you know something? – even in my own movies, the ones I directed, no one was ever a weatherman! In the future, I should totally make a weatherman movie. Just for the hell of it, man. What's next? *Joint Venture*. 1977. I'm sure I had a few joints on that set! *Here Comes the Bride* (1978). Samantha Fox. It was about a bride. There was probably a wedding scene? I don't know. I have no idea. *Final Test*. 1978. Don't remember it...

Wait... Yes! *Final Test*. Vanessa del Rio. Small movie. I'm sure I had a great sex scene with her. She was tremendous.

In fact, like a month ago, I was interviewed by Showtime, and their main interest was in Vanessa del Rio. She was probably one of the biggest stars of the '70s, you know, and they were really looking for information about her. I guess, they found out that we did some live shows together. Just me and her. Someone would rent a club or something, and we would have sex on stage. She'd do a little striptease to start. And then, she'd probably give me head, or I'd give her head. With me, it's always about the head! The fucking is always like, "Oh god. What a pain in the ass!" Well, when I was younger, I had a lot of energy. But now that I'm older, I only do two positions. I either lie back so they can sit on me, or doggie-style, where I just stand there, you know, and let them do the work.

CHAPTER 7
CANDICE

I met Candice at a strip club. She was fucking spectacular! I never thought that she would want to be with me, man. I just didn't. But she liked me, so – boom! – we started going out.

Candice wasn't a dominatrix when I met her. I mean, she knew a little about S&M and had some idea that she could, you know, tell guys what to do, but she hadn't really thought everything through. She was just a dancer until she met me. This was 1980, and for a while, I gave up my career in the movies to become like her manager. Yeah, I really tried to make her famous, cross her over into the mainstream, and make female power something known to everyone. I got her on regular television, you know, NBC, and also fucked around being her submissive. Well, I was never into being whipped or beaten. It was more about what I called "female worship." The body. The mind. The whole bit. At first, she was Mistress Candice, and then I said, "No! Goddess Candice!" That sounds *a lot* better!

She was from Detroit, Michigan. Tough city. I went there a number of times to meet her family. Her aunt, this big, fat woman, was the leader of a little cult. No kidding. It maybe had 50 people? I'm sure there are many of these little cults all around the country, all around the world, and everywhere else. I never actually visited this cult *per se*. Because I was male, I guess, they never allowed me to see what was going on. But, yeah, this aunt, she was a white witch and the priestess of a white witch cult. They say that white witches are good witches. Over the years, you know, in our patriarchal society, witches have gotten a bad name. A white witch, supposedly, makes everything good and flowering and nice. That's the idea, anyway. I used to say, "Candice, you probably have a little witch in you." We did go to Salem once, on a trip to visit my family, and she was so excited. I still remember us there, in Salem, with our heads in the stocks.

So Candice had moved from Detroit to New York to see if she could make it as a model or a dancer. When I met her, she was living in Staten Island, way out in the boondocks. You had to take a boat to get there: "The Five Cents Ferry." Staten Island used to be all cops and firemen. They wanted to get out of Brooklyn, you know, after the black people moved in, so they went there, and it became a blue-collar white community. It still is, I think, to this day. And Staten Island is where they dump all the waste from the New York/New Jersey area. It runs for miles and miles and all you can smell is poison and chemicals. And then, right in the same area, they built this beautiful mall with big department stores and tremendous delis. Across the way, meanwhile, are these giant landfills, you know, heaps and mountains of garbage. Man, it's brutal!

I got Candice out of there, and we moved to Q Gardens, Queens, into an apartment down the street from my friend Michael. This is before he and Lenny moved out to San Diego. Even later, they would come back to visit us, you know, and stay for like a month at a time. I remember, once, they brought back a couple of dancers. For a while, San Diego was the #1 city for strippers, and my friends, Michael and Lenny, they each started going out with a dancer. This time, when they came back to New York, we all went upstate, and Lenny actually got married. I remember the wedding. Well, I remember *the night before* the wedding! Lenny said that he had some special thing that got you really high. And I'll never forget, the wedding party, maybe 15 of us, upstate New York somewhere, we did a couple lines of this stuff – it had to be speed – and everyone got naked and danced. No sex or anything. Everyone was just high as a kite and naked dancing. I remember dancing with his new wife, you know, who I had only just met two days before.

Anyway, Candice and I moved into that place in Queens and lived there together for almost five years. And while we never got officially married, I thought of her as my wife.

*

We were in some movies together, Candice and I, mostly as part of a troupe for Avon Films. That was really a landmark thing. There was a theater on 50th street called the Avon. The owner owned a number of other theaters where he would show regular, cheap, porno movies. And then a guy named Phil Prince, someone who worked for the owner, he came up with the idea to show these new S&M movies, the original ones, you know, that were being made around the city.

In New York, S&M had just gone overground. Yeah, *overground*, you know, not underground! After the disco clubs, swingers clubs became really popular. Like Plato's Retreat. And then the B&D clubs opened. Bondage and Discipline. It's called a few different things: B&D, S&M, fetish, female domination, female worship. So here were these clubs, all of a sudden, and there were also dungeons with professional mistresses. This was the first time that you could walk into a club, see a mistress dressed up in her leather, and some guy, you know, in a collar, on a leash. She would drag him into the club from the outside and then beat the shit out of him. Tie him up, whip him, and he would become like her submissive slave. Totally under her control. There were also the masters, men who would dominate women. Bullwhips. I saw all kinds of shit in the clubs. This was the first time when people could say, "Yeah, I'm into this," you know, and meet other people who were into it, too.

As a matter of fact, when I first encountered S&M, I was totally enthralled. I had always been on the lookout for dominant women, so when these clubs appeared, I thought to myself, "Wow! This is really fucking interesting." I remember paying $20 to attend an early S&M demonstration by this lady who called herself Belle de Jour. She looked

70 years old and was dressed in a classic dominatrix outfit. There were a bunch of guys on the floor, all around her, worshipping at her feet. Foot worship was a big thing. It still is! When you're doing the feet, you know, you're at the bottom, and the woman is at the top. So there I was, watching these guys at the feet of Belle de Jour, and I remember getting really excited. I mean, it's not like I wanted to kiss this 70-year-old lady's feet, eat her out, or anything like that. No, but the whole ritual aspect had me very curious.

We went to the S&M clubs all the time, Candice and I, and also did a number of shows with other mistresses, you know, her friends. There was Duchess Von Stern. And Alan Adrian. They called him "Spike," and he would get the shit whipped out of him. Big time! He liked to have his cock smashed until he was bleeding and shit. Personally, I didn't mind having my cock tied up and just whacked with a hand. Basically, it was the tension and the pressure. That's what I was into. Tension. Pressure. Plus, I would have this big hard-on, and everyone would be staring right at it! So that's what I would do in the S&M shows. But when they weren't doing shows in the clubs, the mistresses would work in the dungeons. Or customers would come to them. Like after the first year or so, Candice stopped going to the dungeons and worked out of our house. There had to be a guard, obviously, for protection, so I was the guard!

And we met all kinds of weirdos in that world. Great story. Candice was working at a session place. Men would get her number mostly through *Screw*, and they'd pay a couple hundred bucks for an hour. One time, this orthodox Jew came in. Into a domination place, you know, *to get abused!* The dominatrices wouldn't have regular sex. Never. They didn't even really show anything! I mean, Candice would show her tits because they were amazing. Nice and big. People loved them, and she liked to show them off. But most of the mistresses stayed totally dressed. And this Jew, he said, "The only time I can ever have sex is when we're trying to have a kid." Even then, according to him, they would cut a hole in a sheet. And then with all of his clothes still on, he would stick his dick through the hole. To have sex. Through a hole in a sheet!

Anyway, you can see, even within the already fringe world of porn, I started getting into some weirder stuff. Well, unique. Different. Of course, I was always into worshipping women. I liked any sex where the woman was aggressive, aggressive, aggressive. I wanted them to lead. I never wanted them to be passive, you know, where I'd have to throw them down on the bed or any of the typical chauvinist bullshit. I mean, if I was called on to do a scene like that – and here and there I was – then I would do it. I'd have to really force myself. Be a real actor. And every once in a while, I would fail, you know, I couldn't do the "pop shot." Don't forget, at this time, there aren't any drugs like Viagra. You had to do it all on your own. The whole business changed when Viagra came along. But that was the '90s. That's not this time period! I'm going to show some discipline and stay off of that for now, thank you very much.

*

Right! Let me get back to the Avon. So Phil Prince started producing movies of his own, and after we met, I wrote some stupid little scripts for him. Of course, I introduced him to Candice right away, and he put her in a number of movies. As a matter of fact, she pissed on me in *House of Sin*. Everyone thought that was like the worst, you know, most incredible, wild thing ever! That was the first time I ever did that *on screen*. And I didn't do it again for years. It's illegal, really, but it wasn't back then. Candice must have pissed on tons of guys. And then destroy them! Just whip the shit out of them! I never let her whip me. Are you kidding? I was into worshipping her as a goddess! I didn't have to be forced.

It was Phil's idea to get a few stars from the Avon pictures to do live performances in the theater. After a showing, they would completely reenact their scene from the movie, three or four times a day, every four hours, and the place got really popular. It was the only porno theater I've ever seen where it was always SRO. Standing Room Only! I worked the live show there on many different occasions. Sometimes with Candice, but I'd work with anyone. There was Long Jeanne Silver, the girl with the stump leg. She was wild, man. What did I do with the stump leg? Did I suck on it? Who knows? To tell you the truth, I don't remember. I'm sure there was some kind of kinky thing going on. I was into the kink! I always felt more like a – what do you call it? – performance artist. Even in my other movies, that's what was in my head. I was a performance artist doing sexual performance art. Exactly. So the Avon was perfect for me.

The Avon scene was big for a few years. Some of those original movies were directed by an old-time director named Carter Stevens. And starred Annie Sprinkle. She was a popular fetish actress who did a number of Avon movies and later became a famous performance artist. There was a spectacular actor named George Payne. He was tremendous. And I must have been in like ten of those pictures: *Oriental Techniques, Pleasure and Pain, House of Sin*. Some of the scripts were pretty rough, you know, they would abuse men and women. In *The Taming of Rebecca*, George Payne played the head of an academy where he abused all the girls. Sharon Mitchell played one of the students, and I was her disgusting father. But we were like the same age, you know what I mean? She was maybe a couple of years younger, so they just put her in pigtails or something.

This is the opening scene of the movie: Sharon giving me head on the toilet. By that time, I'd been in the business for years, and I was now into bathroom sex! So it starts on the toilet, and then we move into the shower. I was the dominant, which didn't happen too often, but I knew how to do it. In the sexual playground, I was what they called a "switchable," you know, I could be both dominant and submissive. And I *really* dominated her, and it turned out to be a *really* wild scene! Who knows exactly why, but some scenes turn out a hundred times better than others. Yeah, yeah, we were playing father and daughter, I guess, but I didn't think about that at the time. *The Taming of Rebecca* wasn't based on incest or anything. It was about this academy and this mean guy who ran it, abusing everyone in the place, and it was the biggest Avon movie of all.

I mean, *House of Sin* was pretty big, too. As a matter of fact, Carter Stevens might have directed that one. We reconnected on Facebook, and he sends me stuff every once in a while. He hasn't made movies since the late '70s, early '80s, you know, "The Golden Age." But I think he directed *House of Sin* with that famous last scene that everyone thought was so tremendous. The grand finale! Me and Candice. She had me tied up by my cock while I ate out her pussy. And then, you know, she just stood right over me and peed.

*

After being in the Avon movies, I got a reputation as a "fetish" guy. In those days, that was not good! I started being blackballed from regular porno movies. And these directors who were blackballing me, they were all probably doing tons of fetish stuff in their personal lives. I know they were, actually, for a fact. They would engage in it, sure, but wouldn't publicly say so, for fear of being laughed at or called strange names. Anyway, all of a sudden, I wasn't getting calls from people who used to put me in their movies.

That's when I was really pushing Candice, though, so I didn't care! I kind of got out of the movies while I was promoting her. I started writing those articles, you know, I had her in the magazines every month. *Cheri*. That was a really popular one, and she was in every issue. She had a column in *Stag*. And *Club*, the biggest men's magazine in Europe, they published some of her stuff. I may still have some of those old columns around here somewhere. I wrote so many of them! I mean, sometimes, we collaborated. I would say that 70% of the ideas were mine, and then I would speak to her about them, and she would agree. Yeah, for a while, she was into the whole thing. Big time! Candice loved being a dominatrix. And in the films, nine out of ten times, she would just play herself: Goddess Candice.

She never really fucked any guys in the movies. She would occasionally do women. In the porno business, there are women who don't want to have sex with men on camera, so they have sex with women. It's not even looked upon as lesbianism, you know what I mean? Everyone looks at it more like a photo shoot than a regular sex scene. And if anyone asks one of these girls if she is in porno, then she usually says, "I do modeling." There have been many actresses in the industry, mostly the really pretty women, who just fucked other women. It's kind of unique, right? People in the straight world would see that as gay, you know, but people in porn don't see it that way. Unless the girl is a *real* lesbian. That's a different story. Although girls who say they are lesbians, quite often, the next thing you know, here's their boyfriend on the set.

If they don't cause any trouble, then boyfriends are allowed to watch, or wait, you know, hang in the back. "Suitcase pimps." That's what we call them, these guys who are really just living off of their porno girlfriends. Though, sometimes, I guess, they are also like the woman's protector. Like I was a protector for Candice. Of course, I was also writing all her columns and probably making more money than she was! And still doing movies, every now and then, you know, when anyone would hire me. Those two years, when I was in the Avon pictures, if I did another movie, then it was always a role that had something to do with fetish. Because not a lot of porno actors could do it! But after a while, *that's all* they thought I could do. They forgot that I had done like a hundred other movies before. Maybe more? If you count the loops, then who knows how many movies I was in?

Well, in 1982, I did star in a picture called *Smoker*, one of my biggest pictures ever. It was distributed by VCA, but made by a small production company run by these two artists, a couple that lived outside of Philadelphia. We shot there for almost two weeks, and it was a real artsy, kinky kind of movie. The critics either loved it or hated it, you know what I mean? It was about a voyeur who owned an apartment building. And I played the apartment building's handyman. He was this total peeper who wore mirrored glasses and sometimes dressed in women's clothes. This character, he was like a real pervert. Which was perfect for me, man. I was tremendous in that movie! And it starred a bunch of other big names from that period. Joanna Storm and John Leslie. Sharon Mitchell. Ron Jeremy, of course. I think Joey Silvera was in *Smoker*, too. Yes, I think he was!

Actually, on that set, I remember getting into a little affair with the lead actress, Joanna Storm. Well, I don't know if I would call it an "affair." It was an affair *on the set*. Like you always hear about movie stars, they go away for a couple of months, and the next thing you know, they're having affairs with their co-stars. For months, you know, they're living together, doing things together, and eventually – boom! – that's what happens. Many times, if it was a long shoot, then old relationships would end and new relationships would begin. People had sex a few times, and all of a sudden, they were falling in love. Was Candice okay with this? Candice didn't know. Did we have an understanding? Yeah, I didn't fuck anyone except in the movies. And she didn't fuck any guys either. In scenes, she just fucked women, and the guys, she beat up and pissed on.

Back in those days, if we had the internet and social media, then Candice would have been a millionaire! She was the biggest mistress around. Men were constantly writing to her. They would get her information through the magazines. And she did a little bit of phone sex, too. Not much, but we set something up through this mail-order guy in California. I remember, when there wasn't anything else going on, Candice would just hang out in bed for a couple of hours and do phone sex. Whoever invented phone sex, man, the original people, they all became millionaires! After a few years, they never had to work again. And a lot of these women, you know, they could have a real sexy voice, but be like 400 lbs. The guys didn't know who they were talking to!

It seems crazy today, but back then, you really had to work hard to get people to hear about you. I did the best that I could under the circumstances. I could have tried to get some backing, I guess, and do a little indie documentary about Candice, the lifestyle, the philosophy, the whole bit. Hey, I did get her onto *The Late Late Show* with Tom Snyder. He was on, for years, after Letterman. Yeah, we contacted him. I was just calling around everywhere. By that time, Candice had a huge résumé, and they became very interested. I remember they came to our house and interviewed her, you know, with a whole television crew. And then… we were on TV! It didn't help her get as famous as I thought it would, though, you know, without social media. No Facebook. No YouTube. So the episode just came and went.

I really tried everything because that was my goal. To cross Candice over into the mainstream as a professional dominatrix goddess with a cult of female worship. I mean, I always sort of wanted to be like a cult… well, not *leader*. Yeah, I've always wanted to be a leader. Director. Lead singer. Leader of the neighborhood. I'm just thinking about this now. That's what I've always wanted. To lead.

*

At home, I have to tell you, our relationship was pretty normal. It was very sexual, yeah, especially at first, but we didn't really do much fetish stuff in the house. I wasn't like her slave, you know what I mean? I was just her boyfriend. In fact, like I told you, I thought of myself as her husband. To me, after a few years of living together, we were married. And like any typical marriage, sometimes it was great and sometimes… it was horrible! But we really just had a regular relationship, you know, went to restaurants and movies like regular people.

Watched TV. What did we watch? Who knows? I remember she liked *General Hospital*.

Eventually, though, I think she started to get sick of New York. The city, man, it can do that to you. She had been there for five years already, and that's when our relationship really began to fade. She started doing heavy drugs. Quaaludes and coke. I remember being at this big party hosted by Mark Stevens. He was one of the first male porn stars in New York, going back to the early '70s. He would throw a party like every three months and all the B celebrities from around New York would show up. Anyway, we were always at his parties, and at one of them, Candice got so smashed that she thought Mark Stevens was talking to her, you know, trying to hit on her in the bathroom. And it wasn't even him! I had to go into the bathroom, push this guy away, and say, "Candice, you don't know this person. You're so fucked up. You think he's someone else."

So Candice and I broke up, and then, well, she quit being Mistress Candice and moved to Florida. Her mother had died. I remember going to the funeral in Fort Myers. When they retired, her parents moved from Detroit to the west side of Florida, near Tampa. People from the Northeast, you know, Boston, Philadelphia, Baltimore, New York, they all move to the Miami/Fort Lauderdale side of Florida. Basically, the Jews retire to that side, and the Midwesterners, you know, the non-Jews, they retire to the west side. When I got to Fort Myers, I'll never forget, everyone there was over 80 years old! I couldn't believe it. It was a nice, quiet, little place, though, and her parents decided to move there. But then, her mother died from cancer only a few months later. And then, we broke, up. Soon after that, Candice moved to Florida to be with her father, and I haven't spoken to her since.

That was probably 1985. Because in 1986, the next year, I met Stacy. To be honest, Stacy met me. She saw me performing on a set. It was a Ron Jeremy-directed movie, I think, being shot in a bookstore in Brooklyn. We met up at some bar afterwards, and a couple of months later, we were living together. And then we got married within less than a year. Stacy was just like a regular business woman, but she also happened to be a voyeur. Big time! And actually got talked into being in movies by the director Henri Pachard. He wasn't looking for 20-year-old girls. No, he wanted *women*, you know, in their 30s. Who had never done it before. Who would never in a million years even think of doing it. But he would talk with them, probably give them some coke and shit, and the next thing you know, there they are. That's how Stacy started, and she must have done like 30 movies.

He gave her a name, too. Sarah Bernard. And then, later, I called her Morgan Steel and turned her into a little dominatrix. That's when we were married. I didn't want her to be fucking anyone, you know what I mean? So she stopped being in porno movies and only did dominatrix stuff after that.

CHAPTER 8
COAST TO COAST

I check the Billboard charts every week. I've done it since I was a teenager. That's one of the reasons why I loved living in the city, you know, New York is known for these tremendous newsstands with every magazine in the world. There were three big record magazines: *Cash Box, Record World,* and *Billboard*, and I was always picking up copies.

Who was I listening to in the early '80s? Oh god. The new MTV stars. The Eurythmics. Duran Duran. Thomas Dolby. "She Blinded Me with Science." Of course, I loved Madonna. She's one of my all-time favorites! If I had to name the top ten most influential singers/performers over the last 50 years, she'd be right at the top! From her very first album, I've loved every single one. *True Blue. Like a Virgin. Like a Prayer.* She was the first female performer to do everything, you know, and she kept changing through the years. And I liked her politics. Power of the female! She was always doing rebellious things and getting herself into some kind of controversy. The "Like a Prayer" video, you know, was like a big statement about race and religion. There was sex in a church, I think, and she was in love with a black guy? I can't remember the exact story.

I still like female pop singers quite a bit. Most men my age, they don't like the female singers. C'mon. Are you kidding? But I grew up on the 45 pop hits, and I stuck with those hooks, man. Of the singers that are out now, I don't like Taylor Swift. I think she's a big fake. I love Rihanna! She takes chances. Rihanna will do a little synthesized song, you know, but then she'll do some song with a heavy message. She just put out a song called "American Oxygen" about all the troubles in our country, and the video mixes together demonstrations from the '60s and '70s and today. It's been out for like a month and hasn't even cracked the Top 50. But then, she'll put out some song with a simple beat and a little hook, and – boom! – it'll go straight to #1. She's also a big pothead. I've seen her smoking pot in many videos. Which, of course, I enjoy!

Man, I wanted to be a singer. Classic story. Growing up, we always had these huge yards, and my parents made me cut the grass. That was one thing I could do okay. And while I was mowing, I would sing, you know, make up songs, or take pop songs and try to come up with cool cover versions. I would think to myself, "When I get older, maybe I'll do a remake, and it'll be a big hit!" I'll never forget, this one time, years after it came out, singing to myself Bobby Darin's "Dream Lover." I loved that song! So here I was, up on the riding mower, singing "Dream Lover," imagining myself making a famous cover... and I ran right over the bushes and crashed into the house.

*

When we're kids, I guess, everyone kind of wants to be an entertainer when they grow up. And, in a way, I did. I was never a good singer, but I ended up making movies, yeah, movies with sex in them, and that's definitely entertainment.

In the Avon films, I was only an actor and a writer. I had nothing to do with the producing, or casting, or anything like that. And these were still *films*. It wasn't until 1982-83 that the first videos started coming out. Around that time, I introduced Candice to Grand Matriarch Janet, this woman who published dominatrix magazines. She had more dominatrix magazines in the bookstores than anyone. I called her up and said, "I have the best looking dominatrix in the whole country. Do you want her in your magazine? I think you do." So I brought Candice down there, and she put her on the covers immediately. From there, the Grand Matriarch hooked me up with the Printers, you know, who were now starting to make porno movies on *video*. I had told her that I wanted to direct, and she called me one day and said, "I talked them into giving you a shot." I said, "Really? Tremendous! I've got an idea for a script!"

And that was the script for *Secluded Passion*, you know, the movie where I reversed the typical roles for men and women. That idea was ready to go. I had been thinking of directing and was hoping to somehow get the chance. Especially when everything went from film to video because many of the old filmmakers had left the business. Some of them went to work for the new video companies, but I'd say that 80% of the film directors did not become big video directors. Hardly any. Henri Pachard made videos, you know, he made the transfer, but there were very few who did. So I got my opportunity! My first gig was *Secluded Passion,* and from there, I started directing for the Printers. Their distribution company was called Model Books. But a sister company, the one that made videos, that was Coast to Coast, you know, the company I ended up running a few years later.

I have to tell you, before I worked for Coast to Coast, when I started directing, I was one of the first people in the business to do interracial movies. In New York, there was me and the Dark Brothers. The Printers came to me and said, "We just made a movie called *Hot Chocolate*, and it's all black." And I go, "Yeah." They said, "It sold a ton and didn't cost us anything." And I go, "Yeah." They said, "We want you to do the same thing." And I go, "I can't. In my experience working with black men, most of them can't keep a hard-on. I'm not waiting around seven hours on the set for a guy to cum." But I go, "I'll tell you what I will do. I will shoot *white guys* with black women. I don't see too many of those movies around and I think they'll sell just as much." So I started doing these interracial pictures. The Dark Brothers had the bigger budgets and more promotion, but my movies would go out to the new California companies: VCA, L. A. Video, places like that.

No, my interest in interracial movies didn't really have to do with anything political. For me, it was a job, you know, to show that I could direct, and certainly, at the time, I was not given much creative leeway. They would come up with the titles, you know, these crazy names like *Hot Fudge, Black Girls in Heat, Black Sister/White Brother*. As a matter of fact, I would show up with my stupid 15-page script, and the producer would go over the whole thing with me. Line by line! This is for like a stupid little picture, you know what I mean? But it was good experience. At the same time, I also helped Grand Matriarch Janet make fetish movies for the Printers. They were cheap you know, because there was no sex, so the actors got paid less. Now, it's completely different, but in the early '80s, when fetish movies first came out, they sold for just as much and had a longer shelf life. Because there really weren't many of them on the market.

I also made a handful of regular movies. There was hardly anyone left in New York, so I brought in talent from other cities. I remember seeing a centerfold in *Oui* magazine, some *Playboy* spinoff. Her name was Britt Morgan and she was from Tennessee. I brought her to New York with another girl from California and shot a picture called Bad Attitude. That's actually how I got the job at Coast to Coast. When I went in to see the box cover, I said to the boss: "Look at this. This is the worst box cover I've ever seen! I brought in two great-looking girls from out of town. You paid for it, and look how horrible this is!" He pointed to a woman asleep at her desk. At like 2:00 in the afternoon! This drug addict here, Jackie Junkie, was making my box covers. I told him right there, "Let me run the company. I'll come in everyday. I'm not on drugs. I won't fall asleep! I'll even direct for you once in a while."

I needed the work, man. I was just married, and there wasn't a lot of work left in New York. So the boss thought about it, and a few days later, he gave me the job. And when I took over, the movies improved. Everything improved! We started selling tons of product, you know, and Coast to Coast became like the 3rd biggest company in the country. There were a number of big porno companies, but we were the only one on the East Coast. Something we did – that they've started up again recently – is takeoffs of movies and television shows. Let's say, *Dances with Wolves*. We called it *Dances with Foxes*. We changed *The Addams Family* to *The Anus Family.* We were also one of the first companies to do movies in a series, you know, like *Raunch 1, 2, 3, 4, 5, 6*, and *7*. Not many companies were doing this yet, and we did it on a regular basis. I was always coming up with new ideas!

After I got the job, I only directed a couple of pictures myself. Right *before* I started with Coast to Coast, I made a movie called *Fashion Dolls*. This is 1986, and it was really the last big picture made in New York City. I received some backing from one of my father-in-law's clients. Stacy's father was a lawyer, and this client was some guy who made pools. He was a millionaire, the Pool Client, and he told me, if we made money on the first movie, then he would give me enough to make five or six movies a year. And, man, *Fashion Dolls* was a great movie! Tremendous. The reviews were excellent, you know, but it didn't make any money. I don't know. The company that I sold it to, L.A. Video, they changed ownership. And the guy who took over, he didn't want any previous product or to deal with any strange backers. So the Pool Client didn't make his money back, and that was that.

*

Fashion Dolls starred many of the last big stars in New York, you know, before everyone migrated to Los Angeles. One by one, all of the big actresses started leaving. The actors were leaving. The producers were leaving. Every single company left. Because there was nothing happening there anymore, man. The whole industry up and moved to L.A., you know, Hollywood, North Hollywood, throughout the Valley, Northridge, and Van Nuys.

Before video, everything was shot in San Francisco and New York. Maybe one out of 30 movies was shot in Los Angeles. They weren't even allowed to shoot here. I've heard that crews would drive out of L.A., fly to San Francisco, and then meet in private, unknown destinations. I also heard that the L.A. cops would pressure the San Francisco cops to track down these locations and make busts. So, in a number of those movies, you can hear helicopters circling overhead. They finally found the big place in San Francisco where everyone from L.A. would shoot, Bob Vosse's Studio, and after that, you couldn't shoot there anymore or you would get popped. These were the Reagan '80s, you know, when he was attacking all the companies. Nonstop. That was his #1 goal. He basically thought that we were all indecent and horrible, every one of us, criminals, involved with the Mob.

Reagan's government, man, they were constantly trying to fuck with us! Because of the RICO Act, they would plant people in bookstores, undercover, and try to bust the production companies and distributors. When I was running Coast to Coast, we had a huge map on the wall. There were laws against mailing illicit material *interstate*, and many states, especially in the Midwest, where those laws were strictly enforced. On the map, we'd put pins in all the states where we couldn't send product. I mean, we could ship to the East Coast and the West Coast, but Nebraska? No way! Florida was one of the worst places to send things. Anyone who sent tapes to Florida would get busted. It turns out, later, in this century, a number of these European companies that have taken over the whole business, they're all based in Florida. Back then, however, Florida was totally off limits.

Well, it was illegal, but was the law right? How many goods will you not allow across state lines? They just didn't like the product. Sex! It was totally repressed, and still is, in many places, to this day. Imagine how it has been over the decades. I like thinking about stuff like that because I'm a history person, you know what I mean? The only ones who never repressed sex were the very rich. They could do whatever they wanted. For the wealthiest people, the kings, the queens, their cousins, all of them, it was anything goes. But the common folk – ugh! – if they started to have any sexual ideas, then maybe they wouldn't do the slave labor that they've been doing for centuries and centuries. And they always thought the common people were too horrible and stupid to handle sex. The upper class, you know, is always intellectual and spiritual and evolved, but the lower classes always need to be controlled. They're animals!

People say that about porn: "It's just animal." Base, you know, even inhuman. But when you're having really good sex, you're using your brain the whole time. And, nevermind, animal doesn't have to be negative. It's okay to be animal, sometimes. I mean, not with animals. That's different. But I never see that anyway. I mean, I'm sure that there have been little things here and there. I think I saw like one little black and white movie of some Swedish girl doing a horse. Or a dog. Supposedly, there was Linda Lovelace, but I'm sure she didn't do that on her own. The monster who was with her, Chuck Traynor, he probably forced her to do it, you know, beat her up beforehand. He was that kind of guy. Disgusting! No, I never really hear of anyone having sex with animals. That's not kink. That's just revolting. You don't fuck across species, man.

There are certain lines that can't be crossed. Like I wouldn't work with underage girls, and really, no one does. There are strict rules. The legal age is 18. I mean, we did have the Traci Lords scenario, but that was an exception. In the mid '80s, the biggest stars in the industry were Ginger Lynn, Christy Canyon, and Traci Lords. She was pretty, and wild, and *spectacular on camera*. From what I understand, her mother got her IDs that said that she was 18. She was only 16, I guess, but looked 20, you know what I mean? No one had any idea. No one even gave it a thought. She didn't look her age, man, and she didn't act her age, either. She had IDs. She had double IDs! And the mother was the one who set everything up! And that's what happened. Traci Lords went on to make a few regular Hollywood movies, but never became a big star. She was a big star in the adult industry, though. For a while, anyway, she was the biggest!

This was right in the middle of the Reagan era, and they actually busted a few guys who used her in their movies. I heard that she might even have been working for the Feds, you know, maybe she made a deal? I don't really know the facts. Traci Lords was always in L.A. and never made any movies in New York. To say, over the years, I have occasionally been forced to do movies with younger girls, you know, 18-19 years old, but I've never liked it. Back in the early 2000s, for instance, I had a series called Teen Land for Legend Video. At the time, I was directing like ten different lines for them. I had my black woman/white guy series called BBG. Black Bad Girls. Or Bad Black Girls. It could be either. Since the early days, I've always done these movies with black girls and white guys. Even though, when I started, I wasn't as thoroughly attracted to black women as I am today.

Right now, they're probably my favorite. A lot of black women have these perfect butts, you know what I mean? Like I love that Nicki Minaj!

*

When video first came out, there was a big store at 48th Street and 5th Avenue. This was like the original VHS store, one of the only places where you could buy videos, and people from all over the world would go there. And half of the store was X-rated movies! And then, a quarter of the store was music videos, and a quarter of the store had regular films. The Studios, you know, Hollywood, they lagged a couple of years behind. When it comes to most technology, they're always following the porn industry.

One of the leading porn distributors owned that store. In fact, through a company called Coliseum, they also distributed wrestling movies and wrestling magazines. And that's why I got back into wrestling! I had quit watching wrestling when I was a kid. It was all so stupid after a while, you know, Bruno Sammartino, bear hugs, this and that. But then, in like 1984, here comes Hulk Hogan. He had his tremendous entrance music played by Rick Derringer. There was Captain Lou Albano and his multi-personalities. And, of course, Cyndi Lauper! She became the manager of Wendy Rector, this huge female champ. So now there's celebrities and rock n' roll and – all of a sudden – I'm into wrestling! My company was giving me free tickets, fifth row, to Madison Square Garden. I remember being so close to Ted Dibiasi, the Million Dollar Man, that I could really see him directing, you know, telling the other guy what to do.

Obviously, I knew it was fake. Well, not *fake*. To me, it was like a play. The performers got told what to say, when to do a move, and when to lose, but there were also little opportunities to be spontaneous. Eventually, they had all these "reality-based" scenarios. Like Triple H married the daughter of Vince McMahon. In Las Vegas, you know, at the Elvis Presley one-day chapel. And now Triple H runs the company with McMahon. He's like second in command. So, in my opinion, it was great entertainment! And, sure, I also saw some similarities to the porn world. There were these "reality-based" scenarios, but it was all set up, this and that, and just the whole atmosphere. Here was this popular form of entertainment, but a lot of people looked down on it. Didn't understand it. Wrestling was for people who lived in the swamps, you know what I mean? Hillbillies.

I actually made a tremendous wrestling movie in the late '90s. Should I talk about it now? I think I will. It was called *Nude World Order*, based on the New World Order, N.W.O., a group of wrestlers from the WCW, Ted Turner's League. They were like three villains. Hulk Hogan – who was now a bad guy! – came over from the WWF, Vince McMahon's league, with Razor Ramon and Kevin Nash. On the show, the N.W.O. announced themselves as this new rebel group taking over the whole organization. So, for my movie, I rented a boxing ring and hired stunt men. Together, with the porno actors, they worked out the wrestling matches. And then I went behind the scenes, into the offices, and showed the owner telling which wrestlers to win and which to lose. It was tremendous! That year, the movie got a lot of – what do you call it? – nominations, you know, for Best Video and everything else.

I was supposed to make a sequel for a company called Sin City, but then politics got involved. A week before the shoot, this new guy came into the company and said to me: "I'm running things now, so I get kickbacks." I told him: "No way. You're not getting any kickbacks from me, brother. I'm not playing your game!" Later, I did end up doing a huge series that was kind of based on wrestling. *American Cocksucking Championships*. I hired women in the business known for giving the best head. Once again, I would rent out a ring, get a big crowd, and have them square off against each other. There would be preliminary matches and a main event. I showed the women in their dressing rooms, you know, and there was an announcer who gave these tremendous introductions. This whole thing was basically made for the internet. The thought was to get people online to vote for the winners and the losers, and it would become a big internet sensation!

At that particular time, in the late '90s, though, none of my people really knew how to broadcast a live event. No one had ever done anything like that before. My goal, when I really got the chance to make my own movies, with my own ideas and everything, was to break all the standard rules. I always wanted to make my movies more of a total interpersonal experience, you know, with behind the scenes and talking to the camera. Plus, I wanted everything to be "reality-based." Like in the *Pussyman* movies, I always played myself. Well, I'll get into *Pussyman* soon, but yeah, okay, we're still back in the mid '80s. Right!

*

1986. I was living with Stacy and – guess what? – I never told her that I was a sports fan. When we were first going out, I wasn't paying attention to sports. I was paying attention to her! And then we got married, and a few months later, there was the famous World Series between the Red Sox and Mets. We had this large studio on the Upper West Side with one television, and here I was, at home, watching the series. The first game, she didn't say anything. The next game, she asked, "What are you doing?" I was ignoring her, you know what I mean? She said, "I didn't know you liked sports so much." And then, during Game 3, *she smashed the television!* Hit it with a hammer and just smashed the shit out of it. So I took the hammer myself, smashed our dining room table, and walked out. I watched the rest of the series at a bar. She knew I loved sports from then on.

That was the greatest World Series ever! I wanted the Red Sox to win, obviously, but the Mets were my National League team. That year, the Mets were tremendous. Dwight Gooden won 25 games. Daryl Strawberry hit like .350 and was on coke the whole time! Keith Hernandez at first base. Do you remember Keith Hernandez on *Seinfeld*? He went out with Elaine or something? I don't remember exactly, but Keith Hernandez still gets $3,000 every six weeks from that one appearance on Seinfeld. I read that on the internet. I was shocked! And Roger McDowell, a pitcher from the Mets, he was also in that episode. Did you see that one? The second spitter! McDowell spit on Kramer, you know, who was with – what's his name? – that fat guy. Newman. *Newman!* Imagine how much the stars of Seinfeld make just on those reruns? Even though Kramer, you know, a few years ago, said all those racist things, and we haven't seen him since.

Seinfeld is probably the biggest show of all time. And, of course, yeah, I love Larry David! He's like a modern version of Woody Allen. They have, basically, the same look and my sense of humor. Dry, sarcastic, intelligent. And spontaneous. That's the way Larry David writes his scripts, you know, he just lets his actors roll. I write my scripts like that, too. And he plays himself like me! And he is definitely a New Yorker. No doubt about it. But then he moved to Los Angeles, so has the whole New York-L.A. thing. There was always a big battle between New York and L.A. I remember Woody Allen in *Annie Hall*, he came out to L.A. and thought it was all fake, plastic, and horrible. He couldn't drive. He complained about every single person. He complained about everything!

He loves to complain. I think he's even worse than me. That might seem impossible, but I think it's true.

My wife Stacy, man, she also hated L.A. She was a tough New York Jew from Long Island. I told you, she had been a regular businesswoman for years, but wanted to be around the X-rated business. First, she became a production manager, and then she started running a sister company to Coast to Coast, this fetish company called Bizarre Video. The guys that I worked for, the Printers, they had originally brought in someone from California, one of their childhood friends. He had been in the "popper" business, I guess, but was always jealous of these friends that he grew up with, you know, who were producers and owners of X-rated companies. So he kept bugging them and bugging them, and they finally let him run Bizarre. He had no idea what he was doing! When they met my ex-wife, and found out that she had been running companies her whole life, they hired her right away, and she did great.

At the same time, her boss was doing tons of cocaine. He would give her coke, too, and she started bringing it home. I wasn't doing coke. I didn't even want to be around it. I mean, in my life, I've ended up doing coke a few times, and it really fucks you up. Big time! Like you can put a little bit in a drawer and say, "I'm going to use this three to five days later." And then the drawer will call to you, "Come get me. Come get me." Horrible stuff! But I was like the only one who didn't do coke in the '80s. I remember, there was a movie called *Sex, Drugs, and Rock n' Roll* directed by Fred Lincoln. He had a whole table full of coke on the set, and everyone was doing lines. That's how it was. Actually, I wasn't on that particular set. Stacy told me. And she was getting fucked up all the time. I would say to her: "You've been doing it all day, haven't you?" I couldn't take it.

I said, "If you don't quit this job, then I'm gone." I had a feeling that Stacy would quit if I asked, and she did. She quit. And then went to work for her father. I told you, he was this big time lawyer, you know, but that wasn't so hot either.

They were always fighting. We used to go out to eat with her parents, and on many occasions, she and her father would have battles. She'd end up walking out of the restaurant, taking our car, and going home. And I had to go home with the parents! This happened many times that I can remember. Stacy was really smart, but definitely had some issues with her father. Maybe that's why she ended up doing porno? That's kind of a common story. I mean, she was only in a few movies, and for a while, it was a real thrill for her! After she quit, though, she wasn't interested in porno movies for years. She didn't even want to look at them! Maybe she felt guilty, you know what I mean?

*

Many different people have written books about their lives in porn, but I never really read them. Lots of actresses, particularly, write books, you know, because everyone is interested in what they have to say. Both Linda Lovelace and Traci Lords wrote these famous books where they denied their whole lives and said that they were manipulated and controlled by people in the industry. Linda Lovelace probably *was* manipulated and controlled. Traci Lords wasn't. That's a bunch of bullshit. She wanted to become famous doing X-rated movies. Maybe she hoped, later, after she wrote the book, that everyone would say, "Wow! She was a good girl after all." Obviously, there is guilt that can set in later. Like my ex-wife, Stacy, all of a sudden, she felt like she had been exploited. Maybe she was, in some ways, but it was her idea. She wasn't being controlled. She was getting off on it more than anyone!

I don't think you can make an exact general statement about this. Everyone is different. But women who later feel exploited or ashamed or regretful, that could just be the old repression kicking back in. Certain women, they might think, "Oh, I shouldn't have done this." They wish they had kept their sexuality private, you know what I mean?

They feel like that about their sexuality because we've been repressed. Everything about our sexuality has been repressed for centuries upon centuries! Men control women by making them not want to enjoy their sexuality. It's been a patriarchal world forever! So that's one of the main reasons why these women might feel this way. I just think that the repression has been so heavy, man. And that's what I've always thought – always – that repression of sexuality is more intense than just about anything.

That and how everyone is always forced into a religion. I mean, religions are just big cults. All of these Bible stories, they are like 800 years apart! Listen, at my dog park here, an event can take place, 20 people can see it, and within three days, everyone will have a different story! So you're telling me a story from the Bible, you know, that happened thousands of years ago, it's going to be what actually happened. The odds are about 1%! One story led to another story, and it's been interpreted and re-interpreted, and that's how I've always looked at the Bible. That's why I have my own religion. I worship women, you know, but they've been used and abused for centuries because men are just so insecure and vicious. Men are bullies! That's basically what men have been doing to women for years: bullying them around. It's only changed somewhat over the last few decades. And people don't realize that. They don't go back. They can't go back.

For instance, Vin Scully, the announcer for the Dodgers, he's like 85-years old now, and to me, the greatest announcer of all time. He still sounds tremendous! I was watching the game the other night, and it was the anniversary of D-Day. Throughout the game, he kept saying, "Folks, remind your kids and your grandkids about D-Day, the day when America saved the world." And he didn't say it, yeah, when we started to become a global military empire. He kept reminding everyone, and at the end of the game, after the Dodgers won, he said it again: "Remember, this is the anniversary of D-Day when we achieved victory in Europe." That was 50... I man, 60 years ago. 1944. Is that 60 years ago? No! *That's*

70 years ago! And no one remembers. When America started to become an empire, going everywhere around the world, getting involved in everyone's shit. Before that, you know, we never did.

CHAPTER 9
BIG TOP

I had seen it all coming. Everything, basically, by my mid-20s, studying history, I had figured out how I was, why I felt like I did, and what I was supposed to do with my life. Sure, I probably picked up some of it on acid trips, but it was also there in my mind. The acid just brought it right to the fucking top, you know what I mean? *Whoosh!* I had a mission. I had a mission to promote the power of pussy.

It felt like a spiritual calling. Sex can be spiritual. The potential is there, man, if the mind is open and free. There's a lot of jungle in the way, though, stuff you have to work through in order to get to a point like that. And yet, there's nothing spiritual about most porn movies. I know that. But I've always wanted to turn my vision into a whole religious thing, you know, show women as these priestesses who tease their followers and make them worship. I mean, I never went full blast. I should have gone *full blast* on Twitter, and Facebook, and really promoted myself. Instead, where it says "religion," I just write "female worship." Besides, I'm not really into social media. Most people in this business are only on there to sell themselves, get famous, and make money. The producers and distributors, men especially, if they heard me, would be totally against my philosophy. They loved *Pussyman* because *Pussyman* sold, but they never actually cared about "pussy power."

I made a series of movies called *Pussy Power*. This was for Big Top Video while I was running Coast to Coast, a little before *Pussyman*. Big Top was run by a friend of mine, Sam Xavier. For a long time, Sam worked for the bookstores in New York, and then even when he ran Big Top out in Arizona, he wasn't really a part of the jetset. We met at a convention, and I told him about my obsession with big breasts. He said, "Oh, you're a punter?" In England, men who like big breasts are called punters. I said, "Yeah, man, I'm a punter. I'm a freak with it!" Big Top only sold movies that featured women with giant breasts. That was his specialty, so we got along right away. He was from New York. And smoked weed. And liked sports, you know, especially the Rangers. He passed away, Sam, may he rest in peace. Cancer. I was very good friends with him for a long time, and I'd say we worked together, probably, in all, on about 80 projects.

Sam and I, we shot little documentaries about the girls. This was after the clubs started featuring girls with freakishly large breasts. I'd see an ad for some place downtown where they had women with 65" breasts. So, of course, we'd go down there, lunchtime on Wall Street, you know, and it was SRO. No one could believe how big these breasts were. And then, the next week, the breasts were bigger, and the week after that, *they were even bigger!* They got up to like 120". Only a few women were actually doing this, and mostly, they were regular dancers, not porno stars. I mean, they might do a couple of movies, here and there, to get on some box covers and make a name for themselves. Our little series of documentaries was called *Personally Yours*. They were set up like a reality show, you know, we'd go into their houses, set up an interview, ask them about their lives, why they decided to make their breasts so huge.

Before then, Sam had never really been on a set. He would buy his movies, for the most part, from this guy in England. But when we got to talking, I convinced him to make a new series called *Smother Power*. Face-sitting movies. The original ones! At the time, Sam didn't understand face-sitting at all. We got along really well, though, and he liked my work. Plus, I was running a successful company, Coast to Coast, and had been a director in the past, so he put his trust in me. We could bring in these large-breasted models from around the country, some really good ones, like Russ Meyer girls, I said, who don't even do hardcore. Because we're not going to shoot any real sex. The model will just strip and then *smother me*, you know, with her giants breasts and her pussy and her ass. She'll sit on me. And that will be the whole scene. And Sam said, "What the fuck? Let's try it."

Around that same time, I met this artist in SoHo named Rene. I just happened to walk by his studio and see the name – "Rene, Rene, Rene" – graffiti'd outside. So I wandered in and introduced myself. He had these big, beautiful paintings of vaginas and amazing sculptures of Amazon women with humongous breasts. I said, "Wow! What's going on here, man?" He said, "I specialize in this kind of work." And then I explained to him what I specialize in, you know what I mean? I asked, "Has anyone ever shot here before? This is like a temple for what I want to do." Rene was cool with the idea, so I went back to Sam: "It's a miracle! Come check out this place I found." And when Sam saw this studio, it was like, "When do we start?" In the end, we changed the title from *Smother Power* to *Pussy Power* because Sam was afraid, you know, some people might think that we were killing women by smothering them. So we called it *Pussy Power*, and put out five volumes, around 20 scenes in all.

For the first *Pussy Power*, I called Russ Meyer who, at this point, near the tail end of his career, was probably 70 years old. Somehow, we hired one of his girls. So she comes onto our set – tits literally out to *here* – and we introduce ourselves, this and that, tell her about the scene. I said, "All you have to do is a strip tease for us, okay, and then just squash me with your tits. Smother me with them!" And she said, "Can I have a drink?" There was a little alcohol in Rene's place. So we get her a drink, you know, and we're talking and rubbing, starting the scene. And she said, "Can I have a second drink?" We asked, "You're okay to drink, right?" Well, by the middle of that second drink, she's now a full-blown alcoholic. *Totally ripped!* We took the liquor away, but she was basically smashed for the entire scene. Meanwhile, we had to like hide her face from the camera and only shoot her tits. But after it was edited, it looked really spectacular. You would never even know.

*

Like I said, when I was running Coast to Coast, I mostly stopped directing movies. But in the early '90s, when I started up again, my main goal was to make "reality-based" features. That's where everything was going. Nobody wanted the stupid scripts anymore. Around that time, a number of new things had come out, little scenes with people who were not really known in the business. Like there'd be a girl, playing herself, looking to enter the industry, and some producer would pick her up. This guy, he would be the actual head of a small company. Ed Powers was the most famous, and his series was called *Bus Stop Tales*. He would pick up girls at the bus stop and then, you know, have sex with them.

And I was one of the first people to make regular feature movies in this style. In the '90s, there were three big hit series: *Buttman, Seymour Butts*, and *Pussyman*. They got great reviews, you know, because they were "reality-based" and used these new and different camera angles. In order to get the most erotic, explicit shots, where you can see *and feel* like the sex is right in front of you, you have to shoot from particular angles. The cameramen from the '70s and '80s, they would just throw two people on a bed, put the camera way back, and shoot straight ahead. Maybe they'd start with a long shot, you know, and then go in for a close-up on the face when the girl is getting fucked. Close-up on the genitals. Close-up on the ass. Maybe bring it out for a little mid-shot. But none of these shots would turn you on, you know what I mean? The genitals were never shot right until the early '90s when we came along.

John Stagliano was probably the first director/cameraman who figured out the angles. He was the creator of *Buttman*. When I saw his angles, I thought, "Wow! That's the way you're supposed to shoot hot action." I felt like those asses were coming right at me. But it's pretty easy to shoot butts, you know what I mean? I wanted to shoot pussy. Which is a little more difficult. I had to put women in different positions than anyone ever had before. So I used – what do you call them? – handheld cameras. Take the cameras off the sticks and walk around. I would usually shoot from corners, low to the ground, looking up, so you could see the genitalia and breasts coming down at you from an angle. You'll see a humongous difference between something shot like this versus something shot straight ahead on a tripod. I wanted to engage the viewer, interact with the viewer, make the viewer feel like they were the one having sex with the woman. That was the idea.

So these were some of the main changes happening in the business, and we were the first people to do them. Me and Buttman. John Stagliano. And I was influenced by his camera angles, yeah, but *Buttman* was about a guy who worships butts, and my thing, *Pussyman*, was about a guy who worships pussy. He was him, you know, and I was me. And Seymour Butts, he had his own style, too.

*

I never wanted to live in Los Angeles. Plastic City U.S.A. In my previous visits, I found everyone out here to be totally fake. The only things I liked about L.A. were the weather and the pretty women. Not much else. I mean, it was nice for a little visit, you know what I mean? Go to the beach. Check out the canyons. Fine. Great. But live here full time? I don't think so.

I had been here once to make a movie called *California Taboo*. Well, we shot it in San Francisco, but the people were all hired in Los Angeles. I was here for like a week going to agents and interviewing talent. The whole time, I was thinking, "Ugh! This is horrible! Let's go to San Francisco now!" We left for the location and didn't go back to L.A. for the remainder of the trip. So when it was finally time for me to make *Pussyman*, you know, after I came up with the idea,

I had to make a business decision to move out here. If you really wanted to make a big movie, then you had to do it in Los Angeles. Immediately, though, I saw that I had better make a lot of money because I wanted to have places in both cities, you know, New York and Los Angeles. I really didn't think I could live out here. But I had no choice. I couldn't shoot *Pussyman* in New York. There was just no way.

I maybe could have stayed in New York, made the *Pussyman* movies for Coast to Coast, and traveled back and forth. But I wanted my own company. This was my chance to do what I always wanted! That summer, I tried to work out a deal with my boss where I'd stay with them, but also start my own thing in L.A. I told you, I made a number of weekend trips to the Hamptons, and while we were talking, he would make the deal. When Monday rolled around, however, back in his office, he had changed his mind. Man, I had been running that fucking company for eight years already and made them millions of dollars. No matter, my boss was like, "You have a great job here. Why do you want to go off on your own?" I had to go! I was in my early 40s and probably in the middle of a – what's it called? – mid-life crisis. I was at that age, you know what I mean?

But I shot the first *Pussyman* movies for Coast to Coast, so I had some big promotion behind it from the beginning. That really helped. Bruce/Will Divide had already been out here for a year and helped me put them together. He really pushed me to do the idea, and we even co-wrote some of the scripts. He had never made movies before, though, so I said to him: "If you want to be a professional, then go to some sets. See which ones are really good and learn from the best." And Bruce/Will Divide did a great job! He found the cameramen. He hired an associate director, someone who'd been directing in L.A. for a long time. This guy thought this movie was going to be a disaster. In fact, the whole crew thought that I had no idea what I was doing. Like the editor would say to me, "You can't do this. You're breaking the rules." I told him, "I want to break the rules, man. I want to break *all the rules!*"

We were just guerilla cameramen basically, shooting from new angles. And I came up with the idea of making a feature movie all "reality-based" and having participants talk to the camera. In the middle of a scene, a girl would start conversing back and forth with the audience. I was the first director ever to do that! And I played myself, Pussyman, the head of the company, and Bruce/Will Divide played my associate. We hired a big name actor to play a detective whose job was to find the woman with the best-looking pussy. If he brought her to us, then he would get a reward, and the girl would become a star, you know, get a contract from our company. That was the setup for the original *Pussyman*. In the first scene of the first movie, I brought in Gene Ross, this big writer for *AVN. Adult Video News*. We joke around a little bit, you know, and then in walks my secretary, Summer Knight. I say to her: "Listen. There's a big writer here. He wants to see what you look like." So she does a little strip tease for us, and then, she puts on the jewelry.

That became my trademark. When I moved out here, I met an older lady who made this particular jewelry that fit around the lips. I called them "pussy clips." In every movie, I would include a 10-15 minute segment of beautiful women, showing off their genitalia, wearing this jewelry, teasing the camera. I used tons of tease, you know, whereas, most of the time, in sex movies, there will be some dialogue and then – boom! – sex. But I wanted to present tease as something new, something different. For one of the movies, I even invited the jewelry-maker onto the set to put the "pussy clips" right on the models. And then actually put her into the movie! I was always looking for opportunities to put something real on camera. We were like ahead of reality television, you know what I mean? In fact, I think some of the *Pussyman* movies were *better than* reality television! That was one of the main reasons why they caught on.

The movies were so popular and sold so many copies that we decided to continue on with the series. The third one was called *Pussyman 3: The Search Continues*. Still looking.

New detective. By this point, Bruce/Will Divide and I had found a backer in L.A. and started our own company, Snatch Productions. There was no going back. Personally, I was having a spectacular time, you know, making the kinds of movies that I always wanted to make. They had huge budgets, over $100,000, with amazing MTV rock n' roll sets. There were photographers and reporters from the magazines. Even some from Paris. And we shot in tremendous locations. Around that time, there was this giant earthquake, so there were lots of California mansions where just like a little part of the house was fucked up. So we would get great deals. Many of these mansions were in Calabasas, fairly unknown at the time, before the Kardashians made it famous.

We were going for this whole grandiose thing. Contract girls didn't become a staple in the business until the late '90s, so I could pick from anyone that I wanted. I searched for a combination of the best-looking women with the most gorgeous pussies. And, after that, you know, women who were erotic, and wild, and smart. If I could find them all, then – boom! – that's who I hired. And we put a lot of *Playboy*-like stuff into our movies. For the opening of *Pussyman 3*, you know, during the opening credits, I shot four naked women washing a car. There was nice music in the background, and they were on a beautiful car, covered in soapsuds. We got so many calls: "Oh, I love the opening to *Pussyman 3*, man. It's awesome!" It was awesome because I hired the best women. Summer Knight was the star of #1 and she had one of the most beautiful pussies I've ever seen. Tiffany Minx was the star of #2. She was on the box cover. Julia Ann was the star of #3. Basically, these were some of the biggest stars of that time.

For *Pussyman 5*, Bruce/Will Divide met this actress named Leena. She was a wild nymphomaniac with a tremendous personality and talked in a little squeaky voice. Leena was the greatest! This movie was set in a mansion, supposedly owned by Leena, and throughout the house, in every room, there were auditions taking place. We didn't really have a script, just a basic outline, you know, and we gave her free reign to improvise. We said, "You can do anything you want." There were six or seven sex scenes in the movie, and Leena, some way, somehow, made it into every one. She was amazing. Running all over the house. Making all the right moves. Whenever it was the right time, you know, for her to come into a scene and do something crazy, she did. And then, after it was edited, everything came together perfectly. As an artist, it was one of those days, man, when you don't know exactly what you're doing, but everything falls into place.

*

For that first year and a half in Los Angeles, I was still married to Stacy. She came to visit me once, for a few weeks, around Christmastime. We stayed with Bruce/Will Divide, but they fought the whole time. She didn't like him. He didn't like her. They didn't get along. So we went up to San Francisco for a week, and when we got back to L.A., crashed with my friend, Paul Fishbein, down at the beach. He was the guy who ran *AVN*. His house was three stories tall, and we were way up at the top. Stacy smoked, you know, and Paul just hated the smell of cigarettes. Anyway, her last morning there, she had a 6:00AM flight, and was up early, smoking in the bathroom. All of a sudden, we hear Paul screaming from downstairs, "Who's that smoking in my bathroom?" So she did not enjoy that trip!

The year after that, we got divorced. It was our eighth year of marriage, and we battled the whole year. She didn't want me to move out here. I kept telling her: "Move to California with me, and we'll keep our condo in New York. I'll make enough money that we can go back and forth. We'll be jetsetters!" But she didn't want to live in California. And she was constantly begging me to come home, you know, go back to my old job. Did I feel guilty? No. To my mind, in this situation, she should have come along. She could have at least tried! Maybe I already knew that it wasn't going to work? I also thought that she might have been cheating on me with this guy who lived in our neighborhood. I think she was jealous of me because, well… I guess, *I cheated*. I wasn't with anyone, but I was doing those *Pussy Power* films for Big Top. I had told her that I was only directing them. Little white lie, you know what I mean?

And then, one day when I wasn't there, Sam came to visit us in Queens, and he told Stacy the whole story. I think that's when she started to look around, you know, get involved with someone else. Our divorce was pretty easy. Not messy at all. I let her have everything. I gave her the condo, you know, with all of our nice furniture. I figured that I would make it big out here. I knew in my heart that *Pussyman* was going to be a hit. If I kept my focus and did everything right, you know what I mean? I just had to keep my focus. That was the key.

*

The first *Pussyman* won film of the year. Best Video. This was 1993. Well, it was released at the end of '93, but the awards were given in '94. As a matter of fact, I just went last year to give some stupid little 20th anniversary speech. Man, the porno business has really changed unbelievably – like 1000% – from 1994 to the present day. Back then, however, *Pussyman* received this huge response, you know, all over the world, and it was very fulfilling. As it turns out, this character is what I had been searching for my whole life. Now, I was finally on my way.

And then, the year after, my next three movies were all nominated for picture of the year. At the same time! Well, there are two different award ceremonies. The one that became famous is the AVN Awards. There's also the XRCO, the Critics Awards, which I won. But *Pussyman 3-5* were all nominated by *AVN*, running against each other. Best Video. Best New Series. Paul, my good friend, you know, I thought he put this new category in just for us. Because we got incredible reviews. Five stars across the board. We were the hottest thing – #1 – right to the top! Like most award shows, however, the AVN

Awards were all basically decided by payoffs. Whoever does the most campaigning gets the award. And that year, Paul, he made a business deal, right in the middle of the show, and really *waxed* me good. I wouldn't speak to him for months.

He denies it to this day. Here I was, at this award show, really feeling like a big shot. Very quickly, I had turned into this cool California guy. My hair was long in the back. I had like a – what's it called? – mullet. It wasn't like a blue-collar mullet, no, but it was definitely a mullet. So the first award is for like Best Orgy or something I didn't really give a shit about, you know what I mean? And we win. Okay. I was going like *this*, running my hands through my hair, getting ready for a big night. Bruce/Will Divide was like, "What the fuck are you doing? Stop messing with your hair!" And then, in the middle of the show, Paul came on stage to make a special announcement. He said, "I want to introduce the head of Private of Sweden. We just made a deal with them, and it's his birthday." Right away, Bruce/Will Divide said, "He's gonna fuck us. I don't care if you're friends with him, he probably made some deal with these Europeans and made a fucking fortune. We aren't winning anything." And guess who was 100% correct? Bruce/Will Divide.

No win for Best Video. No win for Best New Series. After that first stupid award, we didn't win anything for the rest of the night. Yeah, I'm always nominated, but rarely win at those awards shows. That particular year, though, I was really upset. I thought, "God, how could you do that to me, Paul?" He would come into my office, and I wouldn't even look at him. He said, "David, I didn't make any deal. Come by my office and count the votes." I said, "Paul, take your fucking office votes and stuff them in a fucking trashcan. Okay. Fine. I'm not going to hold a grudge forever." Because lots of people, you know, they would hold grudges against him when they lost. He would promise this person a certain award and he'd promise that person another award. But he didn't promise me anything! No! We should of won that year on merit.

Sometimes, you know, when a product is really excellent, it just deserves to win.

There were always so many rumors about the AVN Awards. It turned out to be this big event for years. For a while, they actually broadcasted them on Showtime. They still do, I think, but Paul gave up the magazine editorship like six or seven years ago, you know, when the business started falling apart. The first AVN Awards was in 1986. I'll never forget, I was there, in Las Vegas. It was held in January, right after the Consumer Electronics Show, so people from all over the country would already be in town. They were selling the machines. The porno companies were selling the videos. So Paul said, "We might as well make a big show here in Vegas." The first one was tiny, and free, like 100 people, everyone sitting in bridge chairs. After a few years, however, he really turned it into this whole production. I remember, one year, Snoop Dogg won for something or other, and all of the girls were chasing after him. At the X-rated fair, the one that ran during the CES, I would see celebrities on a constant basis. Gene Simmons. Magic Johnson. Showtime!

I, too, worked to get my *Pussyman* movies onto the cable networks. I also sold them to the hotels. Pay-per-view. Those hotel chains were making millions on porno, probably even more than the porno companies themselves. All these corporate guys, traveling from city to city, far from home. They're watching TV, 11:00pm, the game is over, and they want to jerk off. So they put on a – what do you call it? – softcore movie. At the time, the hotels and cable companies didn't want to show hardcore sex, so we always shot two or three versions. Plus, cable companies wouldn't use the word "pussy," and that fucked the whole thing up. They came up with these alternative names, you know, like *Beaverman* or *Snatchman* or something stupid like that. So instead of cable sales going through the roof, they were just okay. *Cable sales should have gone through the roof!*

In those days, let me tell you, all of a sudden, there were all of these different "mans" popping up. There was Breastman and Legman and Footman. But besides Buttman, I was the only "man" whoever really made it. As for Buttman, John Stagliano, he has had the biggest company in the business for the last 15 years. Evil Angel. He hires individual directors and lets them do whatever they want. He has such good people working with him and such a solid reputation that he's been able to do really well all these years. He's from my era, you know, we and Joey Silvera, we're the only guys from back then, actors/directors, who still get a little involved in the action. Like I said, everyone else has either passed away or sits behind a desk. Or they're out of the business completely. Because the business has basically died. Yeah, the *professional* X-rated business is kind of half-dead, three quarters dead, to tell you the truth.

After the internet, every amateur from around the world, millions and millions of people, they all put themselves on camera, made a little site, and started making money. That's when we went from like 115 porno companies down to 12. They've mostly stopped making feature movies, too. They just do scenes, and everything became so specialized. Our whole world is specialized, you know, so porno followed that *to a tee.* For instance, at the award shows, there used to be only like 20 categories. Now, however, every little thing is a category. Best Blowjob. Best Anal Sex. Best Group Anal Sex. Best Anything! I haven't been to the award shows in a while, but a few years ago, this actress came over, Bobbi Star, and she said to me: "You know, I was just nominated for 15 awards." I said, "Wow! That's really absurd! Nothing against you, Bobbi, but God, I mean, seriously." There are so many categories and so few companies that one person can receive 15 different award nominations!

That's when the award show started to go downhill. They used to have big celebrity singers and comedians and the whole bit. In the '90s and early 2000s. That was the peak. The peak of the adult industry. And then the internet exploded and everything changed.

CHAPTER 10
BONE VOYAGE

When I came to Los Angeles to shoot *Pussyman*, I lived in the Valley with Bruce/Will Divide. He had a little ranch house in the Northridge/Chatsworth area where most of the porno companies were located. And this was right where the earthquake happened. As a matter of fact, a number of the porno company buildings just collapsed. Yeah, *collapsed*. I mean, this was a giant fucking earthquake! This earthquake, it wasn't as big as *San Andreas Fault*, you know, that movie starring The Rock. It wasn't like the biggest earthquake in the history of the world, no, but it was pretty big, and everyone was petrified! They called it a 6.8, you know, for insurance purposes, but I think it was more like a 7.3.

I was in bed with a woman when it happened, a friend of mine, Jeannie Pepper, once the top black female star in the business. Anyway, at like 4:00 in the morning, the house like exploded, and everyone ran outside. That's what you do. You either stand in a doorway or you run outside. You don't stay in the house because the whole thing might come crashing down on you! The next day, I was in this little bodega, and the entire place started shaking. I thought it was going to collapse right there and then. This was my first earthquake, you know, so I didn't know about the tremors. They are like whole other earthquakes! Los Angeles was a disaster zone. All the supermarkets were giving away food. The National Guard came in. Many people lost their homes, and the parks were filled with trailers and tents. Some people just left the city altogether. Within a month, I was down at the beach looking for an apartment.

Even before the earthquake, I needed to get out of the Valley. After 25 years, it sort of felt like I was back in the suburbs. I'll never forget, looking out on Bruce/Will Divide's lawn and it was like I was back in Sharon. Grass and neighbors and the whole bit. I thought, "I need to get myself down to the beach, man!" I figured that some people might have left and I was right. There were tons of empty apartments, nice places, for really cheap. I had always loved the Marina, you know, Marina del Rey, where my friend Paul lived. In the '60s, this place was really swinging. It's near the airport and, if you were single, then you'd go down to the Marina and try to pick up stewardesses. This was years ago, well before I ever moved there. When I arrived, there were just great apartments and tremendous views of the water. The ocean on one side. And the bay on the other.

My apartment had a fucking spectacular view! On the bay side, you know, so I could see the boats. And there were no heavy waves like there were on the ocean side. I mean, you could hear the waves in the morning, but it was always peaceful as can be. I would just sit on my terrace, smoke a joint, and stare. All around, there were these little beach houses intermixed with – what do you call them? – canals. Like in Venice. Italy. Yeah, there were all these waterways, and everything was really pretty. Plus, I thought, "Here on the water, I'm safe from earthquakes!" I ended up getting my cameraman, Frank, to be my roommate, so it didn't even cost me very much. He's a big guy, 6'3", brawny kind of fellow, who grew up in Miami near the water. At night, he used to go drinking at the clubs, so he was hardly ever around. Which, for a roommate, is perfect, you know what I mean?

I really loved the beach, man. There was never anyone down there. The weather was gorgeous, 75 degrees every day, and when you walked around, all you saw was great sand and beautiful women, you know, roller-skating or riding on bikes. Everyone had this relaxed attitude. What's not to love? It was tremendous. And the apartments were so cheap! That only lasted a few years. When people moved back, they started building, you know, knocked down the nice, little three-story apartment houses and put up high-rises. The Marina is now so mobbed that you can't even move. Cars everywhere. But I lived down there for a long time. I remember calling up my mother and saying, "Ma, this is paradise. I never even have to go on a vacation." That's really what it felt like. Paradise.

*

My first girlfriend in California, her name was Lilli Xene. Her father was a Nazi and her mother was a half-Jew. And she was a regular porn star. Lilli had been fan of mine for a few years, you know, would write me letters. Maybe she was trying to get a job in the business? Eventually, when I started directing again, I did put her in some movies, and we started going out. When I lived with Bruce/Will Divide, on the weekends, I would stay at her bungalow in Santa Monica. I didn't want to be in the Valley during the summer, no way, so I'd go Thursday night and hang out until Monday. She was like a... lesbian? Or bi-? I don't know. She thought that she was a lesbian half of the time.

What a unique individual. Lilli was total L.A. Gothic. She would take me to cemeteries. I used to be petrified of cemeteries, but then, when Bonnie passed away, the whole thing didn't freak me out anywhere as much as it would have normally. Because I had been to so many cemeteries in the months before! Also, at one time or another, Lilli owned a hearse. No kidding. And she really liked S&M, so she would drag me to these so-called S&M balls, you know, old people dressed up in miserable masquerade clothes. This was in Orange County, a very conservative area of California. Can you imagine, all these freaks right there in the middle of Orange County? But we did do a lot of wild stuff together. A number of times, we would have wild sex, in the bathtub, three days in a row, you know, and then she'd call me up a few days later and say, "Why didn't we have any sex this weekend?" She had like erased it from her mind. I had to deal with this!

And then, when she went stripping on the road, she would call me up, and there was always some kind of drama. Constantly! There were people after her. This and that. Finally, I thought, "Okay. Enough already." But she was so interesting for a while! I'm a little different, you know what I mean? So, basically, my whole life, I was never looking for the typical, normal, everyday kinds of women. And I brought every one of them home to meet my parents. The only one my mother didn't like, I told you, was Helen Madigan. The Irish chick. My father, he loved all my wild, big-titted girlfriends! Well, actually, he didn't really care for Stacy. And, to tell you the truth, he didn't like Lisa, either. Never stopped talking. She was pure New York! They both liked Candice. Oh yeah. To my parents, she was the best, friendliest, nicest, most easygoing woman that I ever brought home. The dominatrix! How about that?

*

I didn't hide anything from my family, but I also never told them that I was in the movies. I didn't lie. I just never brought it up. Maybe they knew? I don't know. If they knew, nobody said anything to me.

And I still visited my parents all the time, every couple of months, a few times a year, at least. That is, of course, until I moved to California. And then, yeah, I did not see them as much as I used to. When I lived in New York, though, I just told them, you know, that I was involved in different kinds of businesses. And I was! I managed that record store, did some teaching, had the lighting fixture gig with my father-in-law. But after that failed, and I broke up with Lisa and started going out with Candice, they didn't know what I was doing! When I was at Coast to Coast, I told my mother that I was running "a video business." The Mars could call me anytime at an 800 number and she thought that was the greatest thing in history! I was like a big shot. And with Stacy, I was living a regular sort of family existence, you know what I mean? Our last place in New York was in Whitestone. A nice condo with a pool, tennis courts, the whole bit.

So I didn't tell them a thing about being in the movies. Somewhere along the line, in the '80s, I did tell Bonnie. We were at Faneuil Hall when I confessed how I had actually been in sex movies, and she immediately started giving me a lecture: "What do you mean? You're not a chauvinist! Why are you objectifying women?" So we had a fight. Well, it was a long discussion. We were still talking, hours later, back at her house. I understood where she was coming from. I respected her, but still didn't believe that she was right. I had studied all this stuff: history, the repression of women, da da da. She was a few years younger than me, and those years made a big difference. Like Mike Graffone, for instance, he is four years younger than me and doesn't know half the things that I went through. By the time he was in college, everyone was wearing jeans and smoking pot. We had to fight for our freedoms. Freedoms that are now, you know, mostly taken for granted.

I remember, finally, I told my father. No, wait, *Bonnie told my father!* That's what happened. After our discussion, Bonnie went and told Abe that I was in the X-rated business. So I said, "Yeah, dad, I run this company now. And was in some pictures before." He wasn't mad. He didn't give me any flak. This was after he retired, you know, when he was going to college and had totally chilled out. My uncle Danny, my father's brother, he knew back in the '70s. I told him everything. I didn't have to be afraid of any repercussions. I could talk to Danny, you know, and liked hanging out with him. He lived in Randolph, near Sharon, so we'd meet up at night, and he would take me to the dog track. He wasn't intense like my father. My father was *intense*, you know what I mean? There was no way I was going to tell him about the movies. I was petrified of what he might do. You know something? I haven't heard from Danny or his family in like 20 years. I haven't been in touch with his kids or any of them. I'm sure he has passed away. But I don't know. I have no idea.

*

Right at this time, in the early '90s, everything went digital. Clearer shots. Smaller cameras, so you could maneuver around better, and editing was now being done on Apple. There was a tremendous difference. And this is when the first *Pussyman* movies were coming out. Exactly. My previous movies were all on VHS, you know, big boxes, but these were now on DVD. We were still selling VHS until the mid-'90s, because only part of the country had switched over, but we sold tons of *Pussyman* DVDs.

Yeah, everything came together, and I became really successful. I would say, '93 to '97, those five years were huge for me. I was feeling great, living at the beach, gorgeous weather, going to all these rock n' roll beach parties. Sex everywhere. Boats. Cars. Bathrooms. Rooftops. These were like *Entourage* parties! And I was still traveling to Tuscon to shoot for Big Top. I probably I had more action, man, in those years than I did in my entire life. I was divorced. I wasn't really going out with anyone in particular. I let my hair grow out and started wearing Hawaiian shirts, you know, just for the hell of it. In New York, I always wore black. Black boots, black pants, black vest, black shirt. I don't know what that was all about. It just made me feel cool or something. I still wear a lot of black, you know, but when I moved to California, everyone was wearing Hawaiian shirts. And I like Hawaiian shirts, but I still wear the black pants. Well, not black pants. Black *jeans*.

Hey, this is also when Viagra hit the market. And right away, everyone took Viagra. It's speed, really, Rimadyl, made by – what's the name of the company? – Pfizer. They make the pills for my dog's arthritis. They were making heart medication and found out, by chance, that it gives you a long-lasting erection. So a whole new class of guys came into the business who now, with Viagra, they could get it up. There were especially a lot of new black guys. I told you, for some reason, before Viagra, black guys had trouble getting an erection on camera. I don't know why. But now, all of a sudden, there were tons of movies featuring black men. There was also like an anti-Viagra movement within the industry, some people who thought it was unfair, and other people who thought it was unhealthy. It's never been unhealthy for me. Knock on wood.

For a number of years, aside from those little face-sitting scenes, I wasn't actually performing in movies. When Viagra came out – boom! – it was like I was 25 years old. I started being Pussyman. I mean, *I already was Pussyman*, but I wasn't doing the sex. After Viagra, I said to myself, "I might as well do the whole thing." And I did. When I was supposed to do a sex scene, I'd just take a little piece of Viagra. Not to mention, if you smoke a little pot with it, then you really feel tremendous. Everything is so *passionate* and *intense*. That's what it did to you. Well, that's what it did to *me*. So I was 45, you know, on my way to 50, acting again, and making hit movies. Living the California dream. For a while there, my head got carried away. I was this big porno personality, and all the girls wanted me. But they don't care about you as a person, you know what I mean? They care about what you have and what you can get them: fancy car, beautiful house, money in the bank, fake tits, fake ass. Did I mention anything real yet? Oh, what a surprise!

This is also when my sister was sick. She didn't tell me for months. Bonnie had been to Ireland, you know, for the summer, and like four months later, she called me and said that something wasn't right. I said, "Fucking Ireland. I bet you picked something up over there." That's actually what she thought, too. There wasn't a diagnosis yet, but then there was... Lymphoma. I remember coming home to Boston a few times to visit her, and we all just thought that she was going to get better. And after the chemo, she did get better, for a while, even went back to work. Bonnie was such a tremendously hard worker. I think she even started running again. She loved to run. I warned her: "Be careful. I know you want to do these things so badly, but don't work too hard. The whole thing could come flying back." And that's what happened. I came home again when she had the bone marrow transplant, but that was a total disaster.

One part of me was doing so great, you know, while the other part was... I don't know, crying half the time. That was a crazy period in my life, to tell you the truth. I was breaking up with Stacy. Meanwhile, I was seeing this goth chick, going to the industry parties, and it was rock n' roll everyday. And then, at the very, very end for Bonnie, I remember, there was a shoot on my calendar, *Pussyman 8: The Squirt Queens*. It starred my girlfriend, Lilli Xene. We had been planning it for a month. And the night before shooting, I got the call that Bonnie had passed away. I said to myself, "What would she want me to do in this situation? I'm going to do this one for her! I'll finish the movie and then rush off to Boston." Somehow, I made it onto the set and probably worked harder than I ever did on any other picture. Everything was in her spirit. So I shot the movie, and the next day, flew to Boston for the funeral.

I couldn't believe it, man. I had just seen her a couple of months before. We went into Cambridge, you know, she was trying that – what do you call it? – homeopathic medicine. But, I guess, no, it wasn't looking good. She was down to like 80 lbs., and I just kept hugging her and hugging her.

*

So here's a story that I haven't told yet. This is a really tremendous story. Me and Bruce/Will Divide were not getting along with our third partner, the moneyman, this guy named Todd. He had been our foreign sales representative at Coast to Coast. When the original *Pussyman* did so spectacular overseas, he wanted to back us. But then, after a few years, we were all really battling with each other. Finally, I decided to just sell Snatch to Todd, you know, and move on from the company. In the contract, however, I had obliged myself to direct one more picture.

There had been 14 previous *Pussyman* features. I also directed this other series where I would interview new girls for our company. After answering a few questions, they did some tease and a little sex scene. And then, if they had the talent, maybe they'd wind up in a feature? These were called *Auditions*. The idea was to have one major line and then a line of smaller movies, you know, that were cheap to make and cost less in stores. My *Auditions* were all "gonzo" style. The *AVN* writer, Gene Ross, he came up with that term. "Gonzo" meant no particular story, just something "reality-based" that pretty much gets right to the sex. Gene might have got the term from Hunter Thompson? When I was younger, I read a lot of Hunter Thompson, and they always called him a "gonzo" journalist. Well, in the '90s, everything was divided into feature movies and "gonzo" movies. But, like I told you, I was one of the first directors ever to do both, you know, "feature gonzos."

Anyway, I was supposed to make one last movie for the company, so the production manager called me up. His name was Al, but he went by King Tongue. He did porno for a while and had the longest tongue in the history of the world. And he had set up this movie, you know, where we were going to shoot on a boat and take it out to Catalina, some island offshore near Long Beach. It's for tourists, you know, they can cruise over there, walk around, do some shopping, maybe stay the night in a hotel. The idea was to shoot a bunch of sex scenes on the boat – because that really wasn't done too often – and then dock somewhere, shoot a few more scenes. We would finish the whole movie in one day, and it would be called *Pussyman 15: Bone Voyage*. For two reasons. First of all, it was my last movie with Snatch Productions, so I was bon voyage-ing. And, of course, we were going on a boat trip.

But this boat trip was not my idea, and no, I wasn't too excited about it. Not to mention, that very same week, I had a fucking root canal. And then I got ill again. A sore throat, you know, *like always*. Also, the night before the shoot, one of our actresses, Nina Hartley, a giant star at the time, she called me up and said that her mother had a dream. In Nina Hartley's mother's dream, we didn't have any of the right boating equipment, you know, radio, lights, this and that. She said we better have life preservers. Now, in the past, whenever I shot movies for Snatch, everything always went smoothly. So I said, "Nina, don't worry. I've been working with these people for years. Everything is going to be fine." Except it wasn't! This was going to be one of those movies, you know, where everything goes wrong, one thing after another, until we're all sinking into the middle of the Pacific Ocean. That's what was going to happen, and Nina Hartley's mother, well, she warned us!

At 7:00 in the morning, the whole cast and crew met near my house in Marina and drove to Long Beach together. When we got there, it turns out, instead of a 70 ft. boat, there's like a 30 ft. boat. We had 17 people. Way too many people for this boat! And the captain, it's not even his boat. He was just some guy hired to drive us around for the day. He reeked of alcohol, too, and I found out that our production manager, King Tongue, had given him this drug that the muscleheads were doing – what's it called? – GHB. It would make you dizzy and just pass out. And here's our captain, a drunk, on GHB, taking us out to sea. Meanwhile, I didn't take my seasickness medicine until that morning. So between my tooth and the seasickness, the whole trip out there, I was sick as a dog! I stayed up on the top deck while all the talent, these idiots, they started fucking right away, even as my crew was setting up. We had one main cameraman, my friend Frank, and two other cameramen hired to help with the lighting. So they started the shoot down below, and I let them do everything. I couldn't direct! I couldn't even open my eyes!

Nearly 4:00 in the afternoon, six or seven hours later, I began to feel a little better, you know, and finally started to do a little bit of directing. Until... I felt the boat hit some rocks. I tracked down the captain and see that he's now *totally blasted!* I said to him: "Hey, I think this boat might have hit some rocks. It would be a very good idea if we got a hotel, stayed overnight in Catalina, and took the ferry back to Long Beach in the morning." And I'll never forget. This captain said to me: "Listen, buddy. You might be the director on land, but we're on the water, and out here, I'm in charge!" It was now like 4:30, and you do *not* want to be stuck out there at night when the waters get rough. So I went to Frank – who grew up with boats remember – and I said, "I hate to say this, but I think it's time for a mutiny. We have to take this motherfucking captain and knock him out. You can drive this boat. You're ten times bigger than him. He's smashed out of his mind. We'll hold him down. Tie him up if necessary. It's our only hope!"

He refused to do the mutiny. Nobody listened to me. So we finished the shoot and began to make our way home. All of a sudden – guess what happens? – water started pouring into the boat. Smoke was coming from somewhere. Half of us couldn't swim. It's pitch dark, the waves were picking up, and more and more water was coming into the boat. We were going to sink. There was no doubt about it. We looked for flares, but only found car flares, you know, for when you breakdown in the desert or something. And – guess what? – the radio didn't work at all. Lucky for us, cellphones had just come out, those giant ones, you know, and someone had one on the boat. We got a hold of the Coast Guard, and when they found us, we were 16 miles off course! Our boat was almost filled with water, the captain was passed out, all the women in little bikinis and high heels. They dragged us into their lifeboats, you know, everyone crying and shivering. Within minutes, we watched that boat sink into the ocean.

The guys from the Coast Guard, they told us that there were tons of reporters on shore, you know, just waiting for us to come in. I didn't want to talk to any fucking reporters. Not a chance. But Nina Hartley was there, and if cameras are rolling, then she'll be right in front of them. I finally got back to my house, and my roommate was up watching the 11:00 news. He said, "Oh my god! There you are!" I said, "Yeah. I told you about my shoot today, the one on the boat. Well, that's what happened!" The next day, there were reporters outside of our offices, you know, taking pictures of people walking in and out of the building. This was a big story! The next thing you know – boom! – Jay Leno invited cast members from *The Love Boat* onto *The Tonight Show*, two nights in a row, to reenact the whole scenario of what happened on our shoot. If it was me, you know, if I was still running the company, with my "reality-based" thinking, I would have collected all that footage from television, thrown it right into the movie, and put it out the very next week.

But – to make a long story short – they waited seven months, cobbled together what they could, shot a regular box cover in the studio, and then released some regular, shitty, porno movie. The end. I made 15 big-selling *Pussyman* features for Snatch Productions, and that was the very last one. *Bone Voyage*.

III

CHAPTER 11
GOLDIE AND JJ

We went to the dog park today. Me and Lola. Walked the big football field, the whole thing, to the very end. She's old now, my sweet girl, and her legs are a little iffy, but she needs the exercise. So I said, "Alright, Lo, let's see if you can do it." She got a little tired on the way back, you know, and slowed down a bit, though overall, I'd say, she did a pretty good job.

When Lola was younger, and I had my other dog, Trinity, we went to the dog park twice a day, once in the morning and then again in the afternoon. Trinity died two years ago, age 12. I got her from an ex-roommate who didn't know how to treat dogs. We were living in that big ranch house I told you about, the one with the tree growing up through the middle. Well, one day, I walked into the kitchen, and he had her in a cage. This was a big house with a big yard, you know what I mean? I saw him belt her once. He was like 6'6", 240 lbs., this guy, and he fucking *whacked* that dog. Okay, she was a bitch, but so what? Don't hit a dog! Anyway, within a couple of months, Trinity started following me around and left him completely. This has happened on a number of occasions where I end up with other people's dogs. They're not mine, you know, but they just gravitate toward me.

When I first had her, Trinity would try to bite anyone who came near me. I would say, "Give her some space, man." She was part Lab and part – what's it called? – Chow. The ones with the purple tongues. They can be trouble. She bit three of my roommates and even a couple of girlfriends. I warned them: "Don't go near her," but some people don't listen. When I moved here, however, I brought her to the dog park, and within a month, she was totally socialized. Never bit another person. And her friends at the dog park were mostly humans, not the other dogs. So I didn't know if Trinity was going to like Lola, but they got along fine. Lola's part Lab, too, and part Rottweiler. My friend's girlfriend brought her out here from Boston – yeah, my Lola's from Boston! – but they lived in a house with three other dogs already. He called me up and said, "Take her for a few days and see if you like her." That night, I called him back: "You're the biggest idiot, man. This is the sweetest dog in history!"

That was approximately ten years ago, and really, she's been one of my favorite dogs of all time. As a kid, in Sharon, I was actually petrified of dogs. For some reason, in elementary school, I wasn't eligible to take the bus, and I remember being terrified to walk home. There were some scary dogs in our neighborhood. These dogs, you know, they would bark and snarl at me from their yards. Imagine, eight-year-old Bernie, scared for his life! So you could say, growing up, I was leery of dogs, but my father wouldn't stand for that. Not a chance. Right away, he bought a dog for me and my sister. A Dachshund, you know, one of those little hot dogs. He named her Mataxa, after a special brandy that he liked. My father got us this Dachshund because he didn't want us to be afraid of dogs. How was that little hot dog supposed to help? Good try, Abe, but no cigar, you know what I mean?

It just so happened, I got my first dog a year or so out of college. It was 1973. When I was living on Atlantic Beach, Lenny really wanted a dog. He was a tough guy, you know, and he was looking for a tough dog. So we got a nine-month-old puppy, part Lab, part Great Dane. The dog was all black and was named Blacky. But that's a horrible name, right? Blacky sucks! So I called him The Black E, you know, gave him an official title. Anyway, within a week, the dog was totally mine. Followed me everywhere. I don't know. He liked my vibes. And when I moved out of that house, The Black E came with me. We were together until I moved into Manhattan. After a few months in the city, I realized, in that tiny apartment, I was making the dog suffer. If it was a little dog, then it might have been a different story, but a dog like that needs room to run around.

So I brought The Black E home to live with my parents. He had already been there a bunch of times before. In fact, he knew the trip so well that whenever we neared the rest area in New Haven, he would stick his head out the window and start barking. My parents had a big house, you know, with some woods in the backyard, and he got to wander out there on his own. The Black E was in heaven. Around the same time, for a few years, Bonnie moved back in with my parents. This was after she and Stuey divorced, and she brought along their dog, a German Shorthaired Pointer named Heidi. That was perfect! Heidi and The Black E were fast friends. Yeah, for a while, they were a tremendous team. But then Heidi died. Suddenly. A heart attack, I think, out on a walk. She was young, only seven or eight years old. And for the rest of his life, The Black E lived alone, you know, with Abe and Frances.

Finally, when he was about 12 years old, my mother told me that they had to put him down. He couldn't walk very well and was peeing all over the house. Most Great Danes only live to be eight years old, but The Black E had some Lab in him, so he held out for a little longer. Like Rottweilers, they usually live around ten years, 12 if they're mixed, 13 tops. So Lola, she has another year in her, maybe. I don't know. If that?

*

In 1995, most of the porno companies did not care about the internet. Really, nobody gave one damn. It was all still basically about how many DVDs you could sell. And even though I had no idea how to use a computer, I saw the future. I kept saying, "I think we should build a site for Snatch. Immediately." At that particular time, Todd wouldn't go for it. When I sold him my share of the company, though, in 1997, I bought a domain name and put up the first *Pussyman* site: *Pussyman.com*. Summer Knight, the star of the original movie, she ran it for me. Summer was very adept at computers. She and her boyfriend, they helped me out for a while, you know, part time.

Before the end of the decade, when porno sites finally started to develop, there were a few people who knew what they were doing. Like Rodney Moore. He was a computer guy to begin with. Today, his site still sort of looks like it did back then, but he could maintain the thing on his own, so he made a lot of money! The first big internet star was Dani Ashe. She was just a model, you know, posing in bikinis with her giant breasts. She might have done a few girl-girl scenes, as we call them, but she never fucked anyone. Because she was a real person, though, and now, anyone could correspond with her, she got tons of people to her website. I actually met Dani Ashe before she was famous. I remember, we shot her for Big Top, in her office wearing an executive outfit. I asked her a bunch of questions, you know, and then she did a little striptease. This was for our *Personally Yours* series. I think it was the very first one.

At a certain point, in the late '90s, many porno company owners, who mostly had never really dealt with computers, decided to partner up with those dot com people, you know, who after the bubble burst, were all now looking for a new business to exploit. In some ways, this made sense for everybody, but it can be dangerous to give away control of your material. The person you hire, if you're not careful, they could leave you with nothing. That happened to me. Numerous times. In '98 or '99, Sam went into partnership with a group of internet guys and asked me if I wanted to come along. The company was called Influx Entertainment. He was in Arizona, you know, and I was in California, but I gave him my total trust. But these guys were crooks. They took our money. They took our content. They really fucked us over. Big time!

That's when I asked Mike Graffone to help me with the website. He makes custom films, you know, that's his thing. Customers will email him exactly what they want. A certain type of woman doing a certain type of thing. Sometimes they're not even sexual. Well, I guess, it's all relative! For example, he's done videos of girls just washing their hair. Or trying on shoes. Hey, he'll shoot whatever the person tells him to shoot. These guys, some of whom have never even been with a woman, they think it's easy to hire any actress, and that the girls are all *dying* for work. And if it's not exactly right, then they want their money back. What a pain in the ass! Although, over the years, I've acted in a few scenes for Mike, you know, in my house. They only cost like $600 to make, maybe $2000 for three-four scenes. I could sell them on the internet, or eventually, put them into a movie.

How did I meet Mike Graffone? My production manager at the time, Mark Spiegler, now the #1 agent in the business, he introduced us. Mark knew everyone in Los Angeles. And he told me about Mike Graffone, this guy from Boston who loved to smoke pot. That was that! We watch a lot of Boston sports together, and get high, and he's been a good friend of mine for more than 15 years. He is very unique. Most every person I know, they all say to me: "Wow! Your friend is really weird, man." For one thing, he knows that I'm pro-female, so he likes to fuck with me. He'll say, "What would you do if the women took over? Whose side would you be on?" I put up with this shit constantly. He grew up in Waltham, MA where his father owned some barbershops. He also wanted Mike to be a barber, you know, but Mike Graffone likes to do what Mike Graffone likes to do. He's a goofball, man, like me.

Hold on a second. Are you hungry, Lola? Do you want some lunch? She looks hot and tired. She's always tired, yeah, but she had that long walk this morning. And now she's been lying around all day in the hot sun. C'mon, Lola! It's time for lunch! You want me to put on a little A/C? Okay, girl. Alright.

*

I was having lunch with a talent agent named Gordon Rael when he showed me a picture of Sana Fey.

Gordon had an office on Sunset Boulevard, mostly for women who just wanted to be regular models. Swimsuit calendars, glamour magazines, that kind of thing. Every so often, we would get together for lunch. On this particular day, he said, "Here's one of my new models. She's thinking of doing some hardcore, you know, to get a name in the strip clubs. Do you want to work with her?" I said, "Wow! That would be great, man." Well, if you can believe it, the next day, I'm at World Modeling, this huge agency started in the '70s by Jim South. If you wanted to do a sex movie, then you went to see Jim South at World Modeling. Anyway, when I walked in, there she was: Sana Fey. I said, "Hey, I just saw a picture of you yesterday. I'm David." This and that. Da da da. I said, "I direct for Big Top and could shoot you anytime." Truthfully, I wanted to have sex with her. It doesn't happen like that a whole lot, but this time, it did.

And that's how I met Sana Fey, well, Tracy, but for a few years, we were just friends. Until, 1999, we made some cheerleader movie, *Busty Pom Pom Girls*, and Tracy was cast as one of the leads. It was like a five-day shoot, and throughout the week, she stayed over at my house. This was a Big Top production, although by that time, Sam was kind of letting his daughter run the business. Let me tell you, not just anyone can make porno movies, but his daughter, she thought she knew everything immediately. And she definitely didn't like that I was friends with her father. She couldn't stand me! Sam was divorced, so I would say to him: "Why don't you talk to some of the models? You're the person in charge. Maybe one of them will like you? Who knows?" Oh, she did *not* like that. She thought I was a bad influence. I wasn't a bad influence. I was a good influence!

Whatever. I said that I would help direct this cheerleader movie. And weeks before, when I saw the location, I said, "Don't shoot here." First of all, it was near a school. When you're shooting a big movie, why would you want to be near a school? You always do your best to not cause any fucking trouble! If you have five people, and no one knows you're there, that's one thing. We had like 30 people! We had this giant fucking shoot! Plus, I told her: "I know this house. The people in the neighborhood, they don't like this guy!" He had his whole backyard broken up into like ten different sets, you know, right out in the open. People don't take their yard and divide it into sets. That's the only time I've ever seen it done. So I said, "You can shoot in tons and tons of places. You don't have to shoot here." But, hey, I didn't have the say-so anymore, and they just went ahead anyway.

Well, on the second day of the shoot, there were some bad vibes going on. I could feel them. They were not good. Sure enough, at like 12:00 noon, there was a knock at the door: "Police. Who's in charge?" Sam showed them our permits, you know, and everything was in order. The cop said, "Okay. Just don't make any noise. It's Friday afternoon. There are kids coming home from school." Well, later that evening – boom! – another knock at the door: "Police. We have a complaint. Screaming noises. Ooohs. Ahhhs. We're going to have to shut you down." I had tons of fucking pot with me, so Sana Fey, you know, Tracy was somewhere out back dumping it. Meanwhile, unbeknownst to me, some guy had slipped onto our set and dropped off a little white baggie with one of our production assistants. The next thing you know, not only is our shoot stopped, but the production assistant and his drug dealer are being dragged out in handcuffs.

Sam only got a ticket, but we were still shaken up. Tracy stayed at my house that whole fucking weekend, and then, well… she never left. I guess, whatever that experience was, it did something to us. Originally, we lived at my place in Marina del Rey, and later, we moved to Santa Monica, near Mar Vista. She had an awesome little daughter, ten years old, and a golden retriever, Goldie. She was a beautiful dog, man, and one of the smartest dogs I've ever been around. I was ready to put her in show business and everything. When we moved to Santa Monica, we got another golden retriever, JJ, a brother to the sister. And before I met Tracy, she already knew all about internet stuff, so then, after we got together, she did that full-time. Maybe she still did a few girl-girl scenes, here and there, but basically, she concentrated on our websites. We were even going to have golden retriever websites. We were going to do all kinds of things. Yeah, we had everything planned.

I felt very strongly about her. Yes. I loved her. I loved her kid. I loved her dog. I loved Tracy the most, of course, even though she accused me of loving the dog more! Anyway, after not too long, we set a date. Sometime in June, you know, by the ocean. Malibu. It would be a little ceremony, 15-20 people, a whole romantic thing. My premonition was coming true. I was 49, nearing 50, and she was 29, you know, and wanted to have another kid. I wanted a kid, too, *badly*, and really thought it was going to happen.

*

Out of the blue, my mother called and told me: "Your father has cancer." And then, in no time at all, it was over. I don't know. It wasn't like this long, drawn out, thing. No, within a few months, he had passed away.

Before Abe died, I went to visit him two or three times. They were now living in a little condo. On my first visit, he seemed alright, you know what I mean? He was probably the oldest guy ever to graduate from college! He loved studying, hanging out with young people, and overall, was just having a great time. He bought a computer and taught himself how to use it. My father was better than me on the computer, I'll tell you that. And when I asked him how he was feeling, he said, "I can beat this thing." On my last visit, however, the whole time, he was in this horrible mood. Pissed off at everyone. He had always been so tolerant of my mother, you know, but now, he had no patience for her at all. And he was mad at me, too. Personally, for a second, I was a little upset. But then I realized what was going on. I knew him well enough. He wasn't ready to go. He thought he was so tough, you know, and couldn't believe that this was actually happening.

Within a year, my mother had passed away, too. That's pretty common. Two people live together for 50 years, and then, when one is gone, the other doesn't know what to do. Sure, I was worried about my mother without my father around. She was so dependent on him for everything. I mean, no matter what, I was always worried about my mother. The Mars was always worried, you know, so I was always worried about her. Poor thing. It was in December when I got the call. She had suffered a violent stroke and was basically, you know, brain dead. That night, I flew into a blizzard at like 1:00 in the morning. Unbelievable snowstorm. At the hospital, I saw her, hooked up to all those machines. When I finally spoke to the doctor, I asked, "What are her chances to ever be like a human being again?" Right there and then, he told me. No chance. The big zero. So we pulled the plug. The Mars was supposed to last for only one-two more days, but she hung on for nearly a week, and I stayed by her side throughout.

Earlier that year, after the Atlantic City East Coast Video Show, I had made one trip back to see her, you know, when she was still living by herself. But then, Bonnie's ex-husband, Stuey, a great guy, he set her up in – what's it called? – assisted living. Of course, she hated the place. It was in Quincy, and she complained that everyone there was Irish. Historically, the Irish and the Jews don't get along, you know what I mean? Never have. Years ago, back in the ghettos, the Irish picked on the Jews. I've heard that from many people. Yeah, the Irish caused big problems for Jews and Italians both. That's why in the Mafia, oftentimes, the Jews and the Italians would join forces. Well, The Mars still had a few buddies left, but in Quincy, there were only these Irish people who would pick on her. Did they? Who knows? Old people can be just like high school kids. To tell you the truth, it didn't look like a bad place to me.

The first time I saw the facility was when I put my mother down. Well, the apartment was totally paid for, so I actually lived in it for like a month. I mean, I wasn't there very often. We slept there. Me and Mike Graffone. I slept in the bedroom, and he slept in the living room. I had so much to get done, so Mike came with me. Mostly, I needed someone to drive me around. It had been forever since I lived in Boston, and he knew Quincy pretty well. I didn't know anything about Quincy! Here I was, the only living member of my immediate family, and I had to take care of everything. There was no one else. So I just ran from place to place, frantically, setting up the funeral arrangements, and it's all such a blur. I hardly remember anything from when my mother died. I really don't. I remember giving a speech, the best I could do at the time. I remember seeing some lawyer to deal with my parents' money. Mainly, I remember restaurants, you know, going out to eat with Mike.

*

I cut myself. I'm not sure how. Maybe on the can opener, getting the dog food? That must be it. I'm such a klutz! But I'm alright. Okay. Roll on. What do you want to know?

I think I told you the story already, how I went to visit my father, and then came back to California and got Tracy pregnant. But then she was called home to be with her family. Her mother was sick, too, and they were like bugging her to run their tanning salon. So while I was going back and forth to Boston, she was living on her family's ranch South of Los Angeles. Today, that area is somewhat developed, although 15 years ago, it was all cowboy country. I remember visiting, you know, and waking up to rifles being shot off of the front porch. Everything in that house was depressing, and so, she got depressed. The doctor gave her the wrong pills. She started drinking too much. Depressing. Depressing. Depressing. When I look back, I should have immediately taken her away, but in that situation, she just didn't want the kid anymore. Too much shit had happened.

And then this guy came back in the picture, someone who she trusted, from years ago. He went to prison for a while, but came back right as Tracy and I were about finished. I don't know. Basically, she left me for him, and that's how it ended. Later on, we became friends again, and I actually directed her in a few more movies. Even though I loved her, she had a lot of problems. We all have problems, yeah, but she had some *heavy duty* problems. Tracy was one of those individuals, like so many, scarred at an early age by an abusive father. He belonged to this biker organization. I'm not sure if it was *the* Hell's Angels. I mean, I think it was, but in Southern California, there are a number of particular groups who do the same thing. They have the same ideals. The same thoughts. The same patterns of disgusting behavior, you know what I mean? And they take advantage of anyone they can bully.

They killed my dog. Well, someone out there killed my dog. In fact, both of those golden retrievers died tragically. When we split up, Tracy took Goldie, who I wanted so badly, and I took the younger one, JJ. He was hit by a car. One day, someone came over. JJ was in the front yard, and when the gate opened, he just ran out into the fucking street. As for Goldie, she was staying for a while at Tracy parents' ranch. And have you ever heard of the Hatfields and the McCoys? Two feuding families from the Civil War era. They lived in Kentucky or Kansas or some place like that. And they would kill each other, back and forth, back and forth, and still hate each other to this day. Really. I saw a special on it. So Tracy's family, they were battling with their next-door neighbors. One morning, they woke up… and Goldie was dead. So it's not *for sure*, but they brought her in for an autopsy, and yeah, she was poisoned.

I have pictures of them over there on the shelf. Goldie and JJ. That's JJ on the left, and Goldie, she's up there somewhere.

CHAPTER 12
THE PIPE BOMB

Bernie Bernbaum just called. He's coming over tonight, Game 6, to watch the Warriors win the NBA championship. And – guess what? – he's making us dinner. Meatloaf and rice. Tremendous. Bernie Bernbuam, coming through. Big time!

I met Bernie Bernbaum in college. He grew up with my roommate, Michael, and would hang out with us down at the beach. So I know him from way back, yeah, but we weren't really that close until we met up again out here in California. Michael was living in San Diego, and they came over on Christmas to watch basketball. It's a big basketball day, Christmas. There's always a full slate of games. And Bernie Bernbaum offered to cook, so I said, "That's great, man. My kitchen is your kitchen." He made us food, and I got him high. At that time, for some reason, he said that he only smoked on Christmas. He's a huge Lakers fan, though, and soon enough, he was over here all the time, watching games and smoking weed. He says that it gives him "basketball eyes." The next thing you know, he's on the internet for hours and hours searching for stuff about pot: articles, videos, podcasts. *He's like a real pothead!*

It's not my fault. It was Mike Graffone's fault! Bernie Bernbaum would sit at my desk, and Mike would go on and on about the wonders of marijuana. He loves to smoke, man, and knows everything about weed. In those days, he was doing tons of edibles. He even made and sold his own butter, you know, to put in the cookies. Mike had a heart attack last year, triple bypass, so he doesn't smoke quite as often as before. Still, he'll come over for the big games and that gives him an excuse to party. He calls everything a "party." I mean, we just sit here, watch games, and smoke pot. I'll do a joint, or two, and he'll take some hits on the vaporizer. And then, he'll start talking about 1,000 different things, going from one topic to another topic, to another topic, to another. And when Bernie Bernbaum's here, forget about it. I can hardly follow anything at all! But that's the basketball crew, you know, Bernie, Bernie, and Mike Graffone.

Except, of course, everyone calls me David. And Bernie Bernbaum, his name isn't even Bernie. It's Steve.

*

I've been smoking weed now regularly for 40-something years. Yeah, pretty much nonstop, since college. Back in those days, I read tons of alternative lifestyle books, you know, Carlos Castaneda, all this incredible literature about expanding your mind. I'm a seeker of knowledge. And I found out that we only use a certain percentage of our brain, and somehow, marijuana gets into these other areas, the ones that are lying there, asleep, and it gives them a jolt. Wakes everything up. That is definitely how it affects me. Over the years, pot has enlarged my senses and made me more creative. When I smoke good weed, it does something positive to my brain waves, and I just flow with it. I'm not saying it's for everyone. You should only smoke pot if it fits you as a person. But if it's *for you*, man, then it's tremendous.

There may have been a couple of days, here and there, out of thousands, where I haven't smoked. Like I don't get quite as high when I'm sick, and I told you, I was born with some kind of throat problem. Tight chest and swollen glands. Compromised immune system. I've seen every specialist. My last doctor, he said to me: "There's nothing Western medicine can do." I've been on every antibiotic, so none of them work anymore. I tried an anti-inflammatory – what's it called? – some steroid. That worked once or twice, but now, the doctor doesn't know what to give me. I told him how I'm always exhausted, so he prescribed me Aderrall. *I can't take that shit!* It fucks me up. Big time! After seeing so many different doctors, in New York and L.A., Mike Graffone finally told me about the gluten, you know, being gluten-free. For a while, the sore throats stopped, and I thought I was cured. But when I spent time in the hospital with Bruce/Will Divide – boom! – I caught something there, and now I can't get rid of it.

Although, of course, marijuana can also treat all kinds of things. And here in Los Angeles, we have *a lot* of sick people! You just go to the doctor, get a little piece of paper, and head down to the store to pick up your weed. It's so much better than the other fake pharmaceutical bullshit they sell. Oh, I can't stand those pharmaceutical companies! But I love their commercials. They always end with a list of the most horrible side effects: trauma, nausea, heart attack, this and that, bleeding from your ass. Yet every time I watch sports, there are more and more of these new drugs. Have you seen the newest Viagra ads? They used to be sweet, you know, happy older couple, on vacation, hand in hand, watching the sunset. Well, the other day, I saw one with this hot blonde, 35 years old. No guy in the picture. She leads us along the beach, shaking her butt, then looks right at the camera: "Do you like what you see?" I was shocked!

In none of the commercials, though, do they ever mention anything about pot! If it was me on screen, you know, I'd say, "Listen, buddy, when you take Viagra, it's a beautiful idea to do a light pot. Take a little hit, man, and the intensity of your experience will increase 50-fold. I guarantee it. The sexual professor, David 'Pussyman' Christopher."

*

I've always been known as "the pot director." In every movie that I've done, I've smoked somewhere on that set. And everyone knew, if they came to my set, then that meant they could smoke weed, too. Every once in a while, when performers don't know how to smoke, they might stop listening to me. Or get paranoid. Or just do a lousy scene.

Yeah, that's happened a few times. But as a director, like a teacher with some bad students, you have to be ready to deal with idiots. That said, I've met some cool young people in the business. I remember an actress named Alana Evans. She and her boyfriend, they made their own pipes. She brought one onto my set and smoked throughout the movie. I put those scenes in the hardcore version. And then took them out for cable. Nowadays, cable people fucking love that shit, but this was before Seth Rogen, you know what I mean?

I remember, I made that amazing wrestling movie, *Nude World Order.* That's probably my favorite movie ever. Because it was all about wrestling! And this is when wrestling was humongous. Friends would come over, you know, people who never watched wrestling in their entire lives, and everyone loved it! Great storylines. Great characters. Wrestling definitely went downhill again after John Cena, you know, "You can't see me." The stupidest finishing move in wrestling history. What does he do? He hits the guy once. Seriously. I've watched wrestling for 40 years out of my 65 years on this planet, and even going back to the old guys, when all they did was hug each other for 20 minutes, "You can't see me" was the dumbest thing I ever saw. Okay. What was I talking about? *Nude World Order*. Right. At the end of the shoot, that night, we all got high and went to see Green Day.

I must have seen Green Day three times, at least. And somewhere in that era, too, I went to this concert in San Francisco, Golden Gate Park, sponsored by the Beastie Boys. They were raising money for the Dalai Lama. This was a whole two-day festival, you know, with all the biggest alternative groups: Rage against the Machine, Smashing Pumpkins, Red Hot Chili Peppers. I went with a few friends, one of my production managers, John, and an actress named Lana Sands. We smoked the entire time. And I even ate a few mushrooms. I was in San Francisco, man, why not? The stage was way up front, and the crowd went back forever and ever. Somewhere in all that, I had a memory of being 20 years old and seeing the Moody Blues at the Palladium. I remembered perfectly, looking around the audience and thinking, "In 25 years, will I still be smoking pot at rock n' roll concerts or will I be some regular schmo like everyone else?"

On the second day of the festival, in the middle of the park, we noticed this giant fucking tent with these people, you know, in the red robes and yellow hats, going in and out. It was the Dalai Lama's tent. He and the other monks were holding meditation sessions. Anyone could enter and meditate with the Dalai Lama, so Lana Sands and I – of course! – we went right away. I probably sat in that tent for 20 minutes, but it felt like days. Everyone was doing those "ohms," you know, and the inside of my brain kept *expanding and expanding*. I elevated to the very top of the tent. That's what it felt like, you know what I mean? It was the greatest high of all time! Lana Sands got so high that she wanted to visit Tibet immediately. The next day! She didn't even know where it was! That was unbelievable. How many times do you get to meditate with the Dalai Lama? Not too often!

When I lived at the beach, I had this Buddhist friend, Herschel Savage, and for a while, I let him live upstairs in my house. At 6:00 every morning, I would hear him chanting. He would pray to this $15,000 Buddha statue. A lot of the richer people on the beach, you know, they were really into Buddha. I went to a few meetings where they would sit and talk about Buddhist philosophy. This and that. Herschel gave me those rosary beads to put around my neck. He was trying to get me to become a Buddhist, you know, but it didn't work. No siree! Not. For. Me. I only worship one thing.

*

I saw Bruce/Will Divide the other day. I took him grocery shopping and then went over to his house to watch Game 3. He said, "Make sure I'm in the book, asshole!" I said, "What the fuck are you talking about? Of course you're in the book!" How could anyone write the book of Pussyman without Bruce/Will Divide?

We were a good team, you know what I mean? We clashed, sure, but then we found a middle ground, and things always had a way of working out. In his movies, Bruce/Will Divide liked to throw in some humor, you know, little comedy bits, and I'm more of the serious type. I want everything to be *passionate* and *intense*. I want it real, man. But we worked very well together. Without a doubt, the best pictures that I ever made were with him. Those original *Pussyman* movies, all humongous hits, they would always begin with our little schticks. Him and I, bantering, back and forth. Totally unscripted. Once I sold my share of Snatch, though, I never worked with Bruce/Will Divide again. All those years, he had kept his job with Coast to Coast, but when the industry went into the dumpster, they closed their doors, and that's when he retired. Now, he's an art collector. No kidding. He has like tons of these incredible paintings all throughout his house.

After Snatch, still living in Marina del Rey, I hooked up with Odyssey Group. They were the only porno company near the beach, and I signed on with them to make a number of movies. The owner, he loved me. When I first bumped into him, he was like: "Oh, I'm so happy to see you, Pussyman!" And then, of course, what happened? He got cancer. I hardly ever saw him again. He was bi-sexual, you know, and as it turned out, had a lover from Sweden. Some executive for – can you believe it? – fucking Private. That big European company. After he got sick, he let this other guy run his business, and that was the end for me. Before then, however, I actually made some pretty good movies for them. *Pussyman Takes Hollywood. Pussyman's All-American Pussy Search. Pussyman's Escape from L.A.* It was a whole trilogy, you know, a troika, all about me, here in Los Angeles.

Around that time, college movies were becoming very popular, and Odyssey Group wanted me to do a series. *Pussyman Goes to College.* That kind of thing. So I'd go to campuses in the area, walk around, and shoot background footage to put into the movies, you know, to make everything more "reality-based." I wouldn't take a big crew. I had these particular cameramen, you know, guerilla cameramen, and we shot in the quads, in the library, all over the place. If anyone asked, then I just said that I was making a documentary for the school. Or making my own film for a class. No one ever thought twice. Well, at UCLA, they had tons of security. I tried to shoot near the football field, and they kicked me right out of there. After that, I basically only shot at junior colleges where no one cared what we were doing.

We did get busted once! Yeah, we were shooting on some campus. Me, my cameraman, and this actress, Inari Vachs. Back then, she was known to give the best head in the business. So I said to my cameraman: "Wow! I have a great idea. Can you shoot her giving me a blowjob in the car?" He said, "Sure. I only live a mile from here. We'll do it right in front of my house. No one is ever around." When we pulled up, she started giving me head. Meanwhile, he's in the backseat, you know, shooting as best as he could. All of a sudden, there's a knock on each window: "What's going on here?" Two cops, a man and a woman. While trying to pull up my pants, I rolled down the window: "Nothing, officer." The woman cop said, "You're not a john, are you?" I said, "No, no, of course not! I'm a producer, and a writer, and she's a model." The whole time, I was thinking, "Please, god. I hope we don't get popped."

After talking it over with her partner, the cop said, "Alright, we're going to give you a break. Just take it inside." So that's what we did. My cameraman lived in like this old hippie pad. I remember, in the living room, where we finished the blowjob scene, there was a giant poster of Jimi Hendrix. In the end, we pushed that movie as a big reality thing. We had the audio rolling in the car, you know, so we reenacted the scene using the real sound. I had actresses play the cops. I even rented a cop car! That was my favorite college movie. Because I didn't like making those all that much. I didn't want to make movies about college. I wanted to teach college! That's what I really wanted to do.

*

When I left Odyssey Group, there were a number of companies who wanted to hire me right away. I eventually ended up at Legend Video. Jack Richmond, an old friend from when I ran Coast to Coast, offered me a deal to make a whole load of pictures. I could have tried to make my own movies and distribute everything myself, but that can be a real pain in the ass. To me, at that point in my career, it was so much easier to sign with Legend. And it looked like they'd be in business for quite a while. If they paid everything right, then this would be a really sweet deal: salary, car, health insurance, the whole bit. I even got internet rights and a percentage of foreign sales. This wasn't just straight cash, you know what I mean? This was cash plus "backends," as they say in the business.

In the film industry, backends are a big thing. Like with *The Avengers*, Robert Downey Jr. made millions on backends. Let's say, the big movie stars, you know, they might get 10-15 million on the frontend, but then 20% more on the backend. To make money on the backend, though, the movie has to do pretty decent. And with backends, it's always possible to get ripped off. They promise you this, they promise you that, but sometimes you won't see half of those backends. Other times, you know, a company just disappears, and you might not get anything! Musicians, for years, were famous for getting *blasted* on the backends. If you can get those backends, though, like you're supposed to, and still get your cash on the frontend, then that's the way to go. Obviously! I figured, at Legend, I'd get the frontend with the backends, and everything would be tremendous.

The movies that I directed for Legend, they still had my name on them. I had a fan base, you know, people knew me. Well, they knew my character, Pussyman. I sort of turned myself into a brand. The different series that I made for Legend were all called *Pussyman's Something or Other* directed by David Christopher. I think I've already mentioned a few of them. *Pussyman's Black Bad Girls* – BBG! – and *Pussyman's American Cocksucking Championships*. In fact, the first one of those starred Inari Vachs! There was *Pussyman's Big Boob Heaven*. I had that teen series, P*ussyman's Teen Land*, which I hated. Yeah, because I now worked for a company, once in a while, I would have to do movies that I did not enjoy. For instance, *Pussyman's Ass Busters*. I told them: "It's not me. I find it abhorrent." They had me in a situation, though, where I couldn't really say no. In those cases, when it was time for the sex, I just let the cameraman take over.

Legend went out of business three or four years ago. That's why I don't direct on a regular basis anymore. I actually haven't spoken to Jack in over a year. The last thing he said to me was: "Any business opportunities coming down the pike?" I said, "Not really, man. What can I do for you? I'm ready for anything!" He put some away before things got too bad. Not like me. I don't have that business mind. I always needed a partner who was good at business. And honest! Legend, however, was run by two people: Jack, and this other guy, Bruce. Not Bruce/Will Divide. Another Bruce. I mean, he's not that important. He's just important in fucking me over. Here's what happened. Jack had a nervous breakdown and went away for a while. Because his business, the one that he had built himself, and worked on for so long, he saw it dissipating.

When Jack wasn't around, this other Bruce knew nothing about running the business. I went down there for my money, and he didn't even know that I had a contract. When I showed it to him, he said, "I've never seen this before." I said, "You don't think that I have a contract? I've been with Legend for eight fucking years. What do you think is going on?" We fought the whole time, you know, because he had absolutely no fucking clue! He called a meeting with his warehouse workers everyday at 3:00 to ask, "What kind of movie should we make next?" They should have hired someone, I guess, but there wasn't any money. Jack eventually came back, nearly a year later, and I started directing for them again. These were now dumpy little movies, you know, $7,000 girl-girl movies, foot movies, other kinds of fetish movies. *Pussyman's Foot Festival. Pussyman's Fetish Party.* Yeah, I did those for a few more years until they stopped making pictures completely.

Before Legend went out of business completely, they first tried to make sex toys, dildos, you know, novelties. For a while, that was the only thing in porno that would sell. We used to make fun of the novelty companies. Although, over the years, I have had some toys made. *Pussyman's Ultra Pussy.* It was a scale model of a pussy, one of the actress' from *Pussyman*, and we put it out for like $200. Guys would buy it, and if they were horny, or afraid to meet regular women, they could stick their dick in this! Funny, right? But this made some good money for me. And those companies have survived because people buy toys. Single women buy them like crazy. These little novelty shops that are everywhere, they're what became of the adult "bookstores." They don't really sell too many tapes or DVDs anymore, but there are still people who like to look at the boxes. That's why vinyl is popular again. Pictures. Little stories. The packaging is part of the fun!

Plus, with albums, you could roll your joints right on the cover. Especially like when *Big Bambú* came out, you know, Cheech and Chong. Bam! Bam! Bam! Roll your big bamboo on *Big Bambú.* That was 1972. A couple of years ago, I actually saw Cheech and Chong. Me and John – the friend I was with at the Dalai Lama concert – we took my Lexus and drove out to Phoenix. Our idea was to catch a Diamondbacks game and then check out Cheech and Chong. But my car got a flat on the highway, and we missed the baseball game. It turned out, also, on that same day, there were tons of demonstrations throughout Arizona. There had been some incident at the border, and when we finally arrived, people had filled the main streets around the venue. Cheech and Chong spent a good portion of the show just talking about what was happening outside. And then they went through their typical pot routines. Some of it holds up. Some of it doesn't, you know, but I still had a good time.

I wouldn't go back to Phoenix though. That lousy city. Put it this way: I wouldn't move there. If I ever ended up in Arizona, then I'd move to Tuscon. I spent a lot of time there in the '90s when I was directing for Big Top. It's too hot, yeah, but it's a nice little college town. The University of Arizona is in Tuscon, so there's some culture there, you know, art and food and music. Whereas, I don't remember Phoenix ever having anything. Of any sort. Except heat.

*

The Big Lebowski. Have you seen that movie? I know a lot of people who think it's one of the greatest movies ever made. Personally, I love *Lebowski*, but I wouldn't put it in my top ten. I might put it in my top 20. It is a masterpiece. One of the biggest cult movies in history. There's no doubt about that. The Dude and all his friends. John Goodman is so spectacular in that movie, you know, how he can't bowl on Saturdays because of the Sabbath. *And he's not even Jewish!* He converted when he got married, but has been divorced for years!

I bring it up because I'm thinking about that tremendous scene, the one late in the movie, where the Dude dumps his friend's ashes into the ocean. When I saw that, it made me think, that's the way I want to go. And then, this past year, the guy from NFL Films passed away. Steve Sabol. His favorite movie, I guess, was *The Big Lebowski*. And when they showed the funeral on TV, his wife had his ashes in a coffee can! Yeah, over the last number of years, I've been leaning towards cremation. I don't know. Jews aren't supposed to think like that, but I'm not really *Jewish* Jewish. A friend of mine, he just told me about this Buddhist term, "dependent arising." Nothing arises on its own. Everything is interconnected. And I basically agree. Like they're saying about the bees, you know, in the whole loving world, one thing depends upon another depends upon another. If I'm cremated, hey, I could just be tossed back into the mix.

On the other hand, back in 1952, my father bought four plots in Sharon Memorial Park. My parents and my sister are there, right next to each other. And there's one more spot waiting for me. Every now and then, I think it would be good, in some way, to be reunited with my family. Yeah, one part of me thinks so, but are they really *there*? And if I was there, would it mean anything to anybody? Who would come to see me? I thought about selling the plot, but haven't really checked it out. How much could I get for it? $2,000? $5,000? Maybe $10,000? I do need the money, and $10,000 could really get me out of the hole. It's a bad hole, man. Everything's a hole. We all come from holes. Have I been through this already? Black holes. My dog digs the holes. She sticks her nose in the holes looking for gophers. There's the Painted Hole, you know, that place in your mind where you have to go, psychologically, in order to break through.

Is that something? The Painted Hole. Maybe I made that up? It's like the Third Eye. You don't hear much about the Third Eye anymore. You hear about people talking in the third person. And then there's – what's it called? – the fourth wall. Like a while back, this wrestler, CM Punk, he revealed what was really going on behind the scenes. He told the whole story of how the matches were arranged and how the titles were determined. Seriously. He broke the fourth wall. CM Punk. *He smashed the fourth wall!* He called it the Pipe Bomb, you know, when he told the truth about everything, and for some reason, they just let him go with it. I was shocked! As far as wrestling, that was the greatest thing I had seen in years.

CHAPTER 13
GOVERNOR PUSSYMAN

Obama's in town. That's what I heard. And when Obama's in Los Angeles, everyone goes a little crazy. He went to college in L.A., you know, at Occidental. When he first ran for president, he was always out here looking for Hollywood money. He'd make a bunch of stops, and they would have to shut down whole roads. Not the freeways or anything. Just certain boulevards in Century City and places like that. But I don't think he really affects the traffic, at least, not anymore. That's bullshit. Any excuse, you know what I mean? Blame Obama for the traffic? C'mon. It's Los Angeles!

To be honest, Obama has disappointed me as a president. I knew that he was more moderate than people thought. But I was listening. I mean, he's one of the best speakers ever, and he got me. Easily. With his church-like speeches, railing against the horrible rightwing Republicans, sure, he had me enthused, you know what I mean? I remember being at the dog park around the time that Obama was elected, and everyone was fighting. Right here in the dog park, man, the liberals and the conservatives were battling! I actually met another director at the dog park, Mark Stone. He would say, "Look what your man Obama is doing!" And I would say, "Number one, Mark, he's not my man. And no one on your side would be doing any better, so leave me alone! Let's not talk politics, okay, and we'll be friends." We got along on just about every other subject, you know, music, sports, pop culture. But politics is a big subject. At the dog park, it was a *humongous* subject.

I almost moved in with him. This was like five years ago. I was broke, you know, had just turned in my IRAs, and Mark had this big extra room in his house. I thought, "Wow! This could work." But then, he told me how, in the living room, he keeps FOX News on *all day long*. What? All day long? I can't even watch FOX News for a minute! And he wasn't the only one. So many people, you know, supposedly liberal people, completely changed after 9/11. Like Mark, for instance, he's a rock n' roller. He's made his whole life out of playing guitar and directing porno movies. I said, "These people you're voting for, they wouldn't let you do any of that! Unless you're playing Christian rock and making Jesus movies!" I actually had battles with my cameramen on the set. A few times, they stormed off, you know, furious, right in the middle of a scene. Eventually, I had to fire some people. I can't be having political fights on my set. I'm trying to do a porno here!

And I'm not going to change my way of thinking. They definitely won't change their way of thinking. These fucking right-wingers, they won't listen to anybody! Sorry, you guys. Like Bill Maher says, "Just kidding, y'all." Love you, right-wingers. Love you, Tea-Partiers. Remember my horrible band from high school? Well, this Tea Party is worse than my high school band! They're the most disgusting organization backed by the most disgusting corporate motherfuckers. They've gathered the Klan, and the John Birch Society, and these evangelical idiots, all under the banner of the Boston Tea Party! What a great name for a band! What a great event! A revolutionary event. For freedom. And what's it turned into? This horrible group fueled by filthy rich lowlife creeps with fucked-up egos who will do anything for power. Oh, these fundamentalists, they are so disgusting!

Bush and Cheney, they really ruined our country. Well, it wasn't Bush. He's too stupid. When he was elected – excuse me, when they stole that election! – he didn't even stay in Washington. After the inauguration, he went immediately to his ranch in Texas. Meanwhile, Cheney and the gang, they set everything up. His company, Halliburton, with their private armies in Iraq and all over the world. And what are they doing here in America? Drilling. Nonstop. A couple of months ago, Dallas had like five earthquakes in one week.

Dallas, where there's never been an earthquake in history. Fucking Halliburton. Fucking Cheney. And as soon as Bush came back to Washington – boom! – 9/11. You can draw your own conclusions. And then Afghanistan. And then Iraq. In my opinion, if it wasn't for the war, Bush was gearing up to come after the adult industry. Big time!

In 2003, I wrote an editorial for *AVN* where I equated Bush's fundamentalism with Islamic fundamentalism. I thought they would just bury my article somewhere in the magazine, but they put it right on the front page! And they mentioned me by name, David Christopher, you know, "Pussyman Says, 'Fuck Bush,'" or something like that. I got so paranoid! This is when Bush was king, doing whatever he wanted, and I thought they were going to come after me. I really did.

*

For years, if you were involved in the X-rated industry, then you were not going to like the Republicans. Not a chance, man. They wanted to put us out of business! Reagan, you know, Hollywood cowboy turned Governor of California, when he became president, he went after the industry 100%. He set up this commission with Edward Meese and a group of other ridiculous people. They wanted to prove how every terrible thing in society was caused by pornography. Typical Republicans. The funny thing is, the Republican party was started by Lincoln. Did you know that?

Since I've been alive, the only president that I've liked a *little* was Carter. Well, I also liked Clinton. At times. There was no way *he* was going to attack the sex business, you know what I mean? In the '90s, though, under Clinton, some people – I won't name names – but some people really tried to see what things they could get away with. Filthy things, you know, because they didn't fear any repercussions. And there were so many movies on the market that everyone was trying to outsell each other. So, for example, there was something called Bukakke. It was devised in Japan. There would be like one little Japanese girl and five sumo wrestlers, and the sumo wrestlers would... cum on her face. I don't know. I never watched one, but someone in America did, and he decided to do American-style Bukakke. He'd put ads in an L.A. weekly looking for guys. Then he'd hire a girl and have like 30-40 guys just jerk off on her.

The '90s was also when we had those big gangbangs, you know, where a girl would take on a bunch of guys. For something like that, of course, an actress could get paid a lot of money. Maybe $5,000, or $10,000, if she was a star. Although not everyone did it for the money. For certain people, having sex in front of the camera just wasn't wild enough anymore. It was normal. And to really stand out from the crowd, an actress might think, "I need to do something crazy." So for a while, there were a ton of these gangbang movies, and every time, they kept raising the number of guys. One blonde, Houston, I think her name was, she fucked over 500 guys at once! She had large pussy lips and – get this – she actually cut them off. You know when you're a kid, at camp or something, and you catch a butterfly. And you lay it flat, under some glass, in a nice little box. Well, she did that with her pussy lips and sold them to a fan for $100,000.

Generally, around this time, I began to see a change in attitude. Especially after the Iron Curtain fell, and the Eastern European guys started coming over. They became the big studs and really changed the business forever. When they fuck, they pound the girl as hard and fast as they possibly can. 1,000 m.p.h. Hold her by the neck. Pound her from behind. Turn her over. Pound her from the front. Make her swallow their fucking cocks. When I direct, I will talk with these guys beforehand and say, "Listen, I want a little tease, tension, build up. I don't just want that boom! boom! boom! It gives me such a headache!" I wrote about this in *AVN*, you know, when I had a regular column. Back then, when someone wrote a column, other people would write back, and everyone was debating, constantly. No matter what, there was always an argument going on. And I asked, "Who likes this? I mean, maybe some of you chauvinists enjoy movies like that, but not me, man."

These European guys, they'll do anal sex like it's nothing. And customers want to see anal sex. Which I can't stand, you know what I mean? Unless you use condoms. Most people, though, they don't want to see condoms in movies. It turns them off completely. Customers will complain to the store owners, and the store owners will complain to the production companies. Me, personally, I can't stand the way they feel on me. I've only used a condom two or three times in my whole life. Don't forget, everyone who I deal with is tested regularly. There's an organization, you know, with a president and a council, and they make sure that we follow the rules. Every performer has to present two IDs, sign a consent form, and then, we check the computer to make sure that they're clean. If anyone comes up HIV positive, ever, even if it's a false positive, which happens sometimes, an alert goes out, and all shooting is halted. The whole business will shut down voluntarily.

The professionals, we do everything exactly by the book and don't need government interference. Let the government deal with important things. Fix the bridges in our country! Fix our entire infrastructure that's falling apart! Who cares about porno? No one, you know, except right-wing fundamentalists. There's a guy in Los Angeles now, this right-wing crusader named Michael Weinstein. He founded an organization called the Adult Industry Medical Something or Other. And he's gay. Yeah, this right-wing gay guy came into our business under the pretense of trying to stop the spread of AIDS. Well, AIDS has never spread in our business. There's been maybe two cases in 30 years. And here's this guy, you know, with a ton of Republican money behind him, who wants to mandate that all actors use condoms. Not one person in porno supported him. They don't need condoms. And they definitely don't need anyone coming in and telling them what to do.

He actually got this on the ballot here in Los Angeles County. Measure B. And it passed. By a lot. Because regular people had no idea. They thought they were saving the porno people by giving them condoms. But everyone I spoke to at the dog park, I told them: "Nobody in the industry want this. Once you get the government involved, it's deep trouble. At the very least, none of the companies will want to shoot in Los Angeles anymore." And that's exactly what happened. Half the companies left town. The L.A. film business lost tons of money because of this fucking guy! They've been trying to appeal, you know, but now he has this new initiative. He wants to expand the measure statewide and appoint himself as "porn czar" to oversee everything. That's what they're calling him: "porn czar." Ugh! That's the last thing we need.

*

I actually had a thought to run for governor. I remember, in 2003, certain areas of California didn't have any electricity. And they caught these guys from the electric company, you know, on tape, making jokes and laughing at all the poor old ladies without power. As it turned out, these assholes were the ones causing the shortage. Typical, corrupt, fucking horrible, corporation! They didn't care about people. They just cared about how much money they could steal. Anyway, for some reason, everybody blamed the governor. He was so unpopular that we recalled him and had a special election where anyone could run. I thought to myself, "Wow! Why don't I enter the race? It would be great publicity. And I can talk politics. I have a lot to say."

I didn't do it. I should have, but I didn't, you know, and that's when Schwarzenegger ended up winning. There was someone from porno who did run, an actress named Mary Carey. Yeah, she did the talk show circuit. She was good-looking, you know, so they threw her on the TV. I actually shot Mary Carey for Legend in one of my favorite series: *Pussyman's Decadent Divas*. It was nominated for Best Girl-Girl Series like seven years in a row! They featured glamorous women dressed in fetish outfits, and I always shot them in beautiful mansions where, supposedly, the wealthiest men from around the world were watching. In the movies, there'd be shots of cameras here and cameras there. And the women would put on a show for these men – who you never saw, of course – but they were watching from secret locations. I was way ahead of my time with this, you know, cameras everywhere.

These live webcams are now like the biggest thing. It's sort of like Show World, you know, back in the '70s and '80s, where you'd go into a booth, and a girl would dance for you behind the glass. But this is in the privacy of your own home, so there's more – what's it called? – anonymity. Some girls do it six hours a day, five days a week, and make pretty good money. Personally, I'm not really involved with anything like this. Once, like five years ago, a group of investors approached me through my lawyer. They were in their 40s, these guys, and probably going though that mid-life crisis. They wanted to break into the porn business, maybe get themselves a little action. I thought cams would be their best investment. So we all went into a place together, but immediately, I was like, "Get me out of here!" It didn't look right. First of all, there were way too many women. And they were crammed into what looked like tiny hospital rooms, sort of like a sweatshop, you know what I mean? I do have a Pussyman channel on Streamate, the site that most porno stars use.

Every so often, in-between jobs, they'll do their own fuck scenes. With their boyfriends maybe? Or they'll get another porno star and split the money. I've done it a few times, you know, when I need the extra cash. Sometimes, on a shoot, we'll set up a camera in the back and leave it rolling. Or right here in my bedroom. If a model comes over, one of my friends or something, she'll masturbate for a while and talk to the customers. They like that, the anonymous guys out there, watching. Especially during the day. A lot of these men, they're working out of the house, or they're at the office, in stupid cubicles, not paying attention to their business. All they do is stare at the internet for hours and hours. They'll go from sports to porn, back to sports, back to porn.

Not that anyone's anonymous anymore. Everyone knows what you're up to online. Or they can find out easily enough. Your phone calls, you know, texts and emails, they're all recorded somewhere. You know my feelings about what's going to happen. In my prediction, our government will become a fascist corporate dictatorship that'll destroy everything. It's all moving in that direction. Finally, when we're born, we'll have little numbers attached to our arms, and that will be who we are, the person, until the machines take over. Every year, there are more and more movies like this, but soon enough, it'll be the truth. Forget the movies already! The books said it a long time ago! *Brave New World*, you know what I mean? People don't read as much nowadays, though, and every new technology squashes words. The kids, they don't want to see any words at all. Only pictures. To read, you have to imagine for yourself, and that takes too much work, I guess.

I still read. Not nearly as much as I should, but every now and then, something catches my eye. I just read the rock n' roll story of Tommy James and the Shondells. I forget the title, but it focused on his relationship with the Mob. When Tommy James went solo, he was on this Mob-run record label called Roulette, and even though he had one hit after another, he never got paid. So that was pretty interesting! Oh, and I recently read Phil Jackson's autobiography. The Zen Master! The greatest basketball coach in history. Such an intellectual, you know, the way he related to his players, taking them to movies, and making them read certain books. Just the other day, you know, someone told me that I look like Phil Jackson. I was like, "What? I don't look like Phil Jackson!" I mean, people are always telling me that I look like Jerry Springer. *And I see that.* Yeah, when I have my glasses on, sure, now that my hair's gone gray.

So I like books about sports, and entertainment, and really, anything to do with history. But someone has to give me the book, you know, put it in my hand. I won't go to Amazon. I don't have a Kindle. I like regular books, man, but there are no more bookstores. Like if someone ever reads this book, if it ever gets published, then it'll definitely be on one of those machines. Everything will be on the machines. It's going to happen. Without a doubt. We rely so much on these fucking machines that we'll become their servants. Like in *Terminator*. Hey, did you see that there's a new *Terminator* coming out on July 1st. It'll be Arnold's first hit in 20 years. The Governator! Tremendous. You know something? He didn't do a bad job.

*

It's true, online, there's more porn available now than ever before. Is that a good thing or a bad thing? Well, it's not all positive. But I think we're exposed to much worse just from watching the fucking deceit and heavy violence in most Hollywood movies and nasty crime shows on TV. Never mind how the general culture of advertising is always alluding to sex. They don't actually show sex sex, no, but they insinuate in every direction. Through bright screens, they pump their commercials into our brains, and that has more of an effect than anything, you know, *subliminally*. The kids, they pick that up immediately. So I don't think looking at porno is really that big of a deal anymore. It's just a continuation, basically, of what kids have already been seeing their whole lives.

Of course, personally, I never want to show men abusing women. So like cumshots on the face… that's not good. Do I think it should be banned? I don't think anything should be banned except for those people who get off being violent to women. There's that famous director who went to jail – what's his name? – Max Hardcore. He had a big house in Pasadena, and I shot there a bunch of times. He was always a gentleman to me, yeah, but I would have banned him right away. He used mostly younger girls, you know, actresses new to the business, and then, he would humiliate them. Write on them with lipstick: "I'm a slut" or "I'm a whore." And make them puke on themselves and all kinds of other disgusting shit. But he sold tons of movies and there were always people who loved his stuff. Because a lot of men hate women. More than anything, they're *afraid* of women, and will do different things to deal with that fear.

I think that's why, in the early 2000s, "teen" movies became so popular. There's plenty of men out there who are afraid of real women and prefer younger girls. For these movies, they would hire young-looking actresses, you know, some who looked like they were 15 years old. I can't stand those movies! What do I care about little girls? Here in Los Angeles, though, more than anywhere, I see older men with younger women. These rich old guys will drop their wives – just like that! – for some 18-year-old. Why? Who knows? Maybe they haven't had sex for 20 years. Maybe they've worked the same boring job forever. Or their wives hate them and don't put up with their shit anymore. Their lives are terrible. No excitement. No fun. All of a sudden, here's this young girl. Even if she does nothing with him, you know, just being around her, he feels better, more youthful, more alive.

I'll tell you, though, when I went out with a woman who was 30 years younger than me, it didn't make me feel any more youthful. Listen, I'd rather not make this into a whole big thing. It's the first and only time in my life this happened, and it's not really something that I'm proud of. But for about a year and a half, after Sana Fey, I had a relationship with a woman named Tiffany Mason. She was 19 when we met, and I was a little over 50. She was part Indian, this girl, and black, and Hispanic, and well, just about everything put together. And taller than me, 5'11", 6'2" in heels. Here I was, this old Jewish guy walking around with a beautiful model. We met on like her tenth movie. And she wasn't this great porno actress or anything. In fact, at first, she really didn't even want to do sex movies. When she was 18, an agent found her at some shopping center and promised to help her become a fashion model. She he was young. And didn't know any better.

What did she like about me? I don't know. I told her right away, "If you find a young guy that you want to sleep with, then go ahead. I'm 50-something years old already and can't be having sex all the time." Do young girls even like older men? I don't think so. She probably liked that I could help with her career, you know, find her work, and maybe turn her into a big star. And I think she liked my personality. We would talk about pop music. She loved the singer P!nk, so we went and saw P!nk together. But for the most part, with that three-decade difference, there wasn't much else to talk about. It was pretty near impossible to have a real conversation. I tell you, she almost burned my house down. Yeah, she left hot curlers on my bedroom floor with a towel on top. Luckily, there was a fire extinguisher in the next room. My roommate at the time, an older guy named Larry Ross, in the business for years, he sprayed everything, you know, and then called the fire crew.

For a while there, Tiffany worked for me pretty much exclusively. I even did a number of scenes with her. Nothing wild. No domination or anything. Just some regular sex scenes. And then I got her into Vivid Video as a contract girl. That's a big thing, you know what I mean? They were the #1 company for years. In our business, becoming a contract girl for Vivid could be the highlight of your whole career. They've had Jenna Jameson and a whole bunch of the most popular female performers of the last 20 years. So I brought Tiffany down to meet Steve Hirsch, the owner of Vivid, and said, "Look at her, man. She's unbelievable! I'm bringing you a huge star. You have to hire her!" And they did. I directed her first few movies for them, you know, so she would be comfortable. Yeah, they gave me some lousy readymade scripts. And those idiots, they changed her name to Taya. I mean, she had already made like 50 movies as Tiffany Mason!

I said to her, "Don't screw this up. I got you a great fucking gig!" But then she was always late for shoots, and finally, they just got sick of her. Well… something happened. I wasn't directing the picture, so I don't know anything for sure. Whatever happened, that was the end of her career. This was 2003, right around the time that I thought about running for governor, so I haven't seen her in 12 years. She must be now 33 years old.

*

By the way, have you seen this new Pope? He came out of nowhere. I mean, he's from Argentina. I know. But they usually choose these rough and tough, European, conservative, kind of popes. The last pope was a Nazi, right? And now they've brought this radical South American into the Vatican! I don't know what they were thinking, man. They were trying to be hip, I guess. It's unbelievable. He says things, you know, that no Pope would ever say. Not in a million years. I heard him say that global warming is real! What? And I heard him say shit about redistributing the wealth! And that real Christians don't carry guns! He's like the Obama of Popes, but better, you know, because he can say whatever he wants.

Of course, the Pope has the best platform in the world! He goes everywhere, and whatever he says gets picked up immediately. Everyone's like, "Wow! Did you hear what the Pope said?" I'm a little jealous, you know what I mean? It would be tremendous to have a platform like that. Which is why I really regret not running for governor. I was popular then, you know, and my friends were all excited about the idea. It's what I've always wanted, to crossover, get my message out, and this was my chance. But when the time came... I chickened out. That was a huge mistake on my part. It would have been great publicity, too, talking my game on MSNBC. I could have been "That porno guy who ran for governor." I could have appointed Mike Graffone as my Lt. Governor, you know, or put him in charge of pot. Secretary of Marijuana. *Find me everything there is to know!*

For the last few months, Mike's been working as a trimmer in this little pot warehouse. He's the oldest one there. Everyone else is in their 20s, you know, looking to be Hollywood actors. Since this job, he's developed a new favorite word: "Gibson." That's what these kids yell out whenever he says something objectionable: "Gibson! Gibson! Gibson!" And now, he can't stop saying it himself. If something is offensive, I guess, then you call it a "Gibson." Or if someone is being offensive, then they *are* a "Gibson." In today's world, we sure have a lot of "Gibsons"! But some people get carried away. Like the previous mayor of New York City, he tried to ban those Big Gulps that you buy at the convenient store. Why? Because Big Gulps are a "Gibson." Big time! Out here in Los Angeles, though, everyone gulps! We gulp soda, you know, in our giant cars, gulping gasoline, speeding through the streets, trying to beat each other to the next light.

I think it comes from Mel Gibson. So if you say or do something offensive, then you are being like Mel Gibson. Because he became this total alcoholic and threatened to beat up his girlfriend over the telephone. And when he was drunk, he attacked gay people, and black people, and Jews, and would say horrible things about pretty much everyone. His father, you know, was some sort of Nazi preacher in Australia. Earlier in his career, like around *Lethal Weapon* and *Thunderdome*, I remember hearing Mel Gibson interviewed, and he said how his father was this piece of shit. And the next thing you know, he's the same way. Maybe not quite as bad, but deep down, it probably fucked him up, being initiated with that Hitler shit. And he made some good movies, too. I didn't really like his Jesus movie, no, but I loved the one after, *Apocalypto*. Oh yeah! I've seen it multiple times. Tremendous.

CHAPTER 14

LEGEND

Is this stuff dripping? It's hemorrhoid cream – what's it called? – Preparation H. Once in a while, I'll put some of this on. For the bags under my eyes. I'm really tired today, man. I'm killed. I didn't sleep much last night. And all of this talking and talking and talking… it's exhausting. Because I've had this sore fucking throat for two months, you know, and haven't been completely healthy in so long. And now my car is fucked up! Yeah, they just towed it. I don't know. It doesn't look good. One of the axles fell off or something. I'm still waiting to hear from the mechanic, but I think it's too late for today. They probably can't do anything until tomorrow, at least. If they can do anything at all.

It's a green, stripped-down, 1988 Mercedes. I bought the car two years ago with 200,000 miles already on it. And it works *okay*. Around the neighborhood. To the dog park, you know what I mean? But if I ever go to the beach, or out to a party, wherever, then someone comes and picks me up. I'm always the passenger. Back when I lived in New York, my wives always drove me everywhere. I'm not a bad driver. I just drive slow. Out here, though, in Los Angeles, they drive like maniacs. Even when I had nice cars, I never drove like that. Every three years or so, as part of my deal with Legend, I could pick out a car, usually a Lexus, and the company would pay for it. Most of my friends, they drove fancy sports cars, but not me. My last Lexus was one of those SUVs, you know, like the soccer moms drive. It was perfect for me, man, because I'm always schlepping equipment. On a couple of shoots, I actually taped a sign to the side of my car that said: "soccer mom." Everyone thought that was tremendous.

Can we stop talking about my car now? I've been dealing with it all morning. And I can't even find the keys! Maybe they're with my glasses that are also missing? These are supposedly my "Golden Years." That's what they say, you know, after you've worked your regular job for a lifetime and then you can finally retire. Well, I like my job and I hate these fucking "Golden Years"! You just get more sick and more injured and your back hurts more every fucking day! I really should go see an orthopedist, and now, on Medicare, I finally have the insurance to cover it. I didn't have health insurance for a long time. When Legend stopped paying for it, I tried to stay on the same policy, but they kept raising the rate. It went from $650 to $800, $900, $1,000 a month for insurance! At $1,100, I said, "This is absurd already." I tried to find something cheaper, but once they saw my high blood pressure, anxiety disorder, and shit, that was it. No one would take me.

Yeah, I'm a real mess! For a while, my doctor gave me some pill for anxiety. At first, I would take the whole thing and sleep for 50 hours. And then I went down to a half. And then to a quarter. It still knocked me out, though, you know, and wouldn't do anything at all. The only thing that helps is Xanax! Or sometimes, a muscle relaxer, like Soma, if my back is really killing me. That's it. I've been to every kind of doctor possible. Specialists, allergists, nutritionists. I told you about my guy, Dr. Frank. He was an acu*pressurist*. With the hands. It's better than the needles. I've done the needles, too, many times, but you really need someone good. I went to a few Americans, and then I saw a Chinese lady, you know, from China. The difference was night and day. No comparison. When first I moved to California, I had a good friend who was an acu*puncturist*. He did the Raiders. This Chinese woman worked for my friend and – wow! – she was really good.

She also helped Bruce/Will Divide when he had Bell's Palsy. I had Bell's Palsy once, also, when I was 30 years old. If someone ever *smashed* me in the face, then – who knows? – it might pop right up again. When I do female domination scenes, I'll say to the woman: "Whatever happens, do *not* smash me in the face. It's bad enough that you're sitting on me!" I love that, of course, but it probably has caused some damage over the years. I'm like an old stuntman. After a face-sitting shoot, I'm totally done. My backs hurts, and my neck hurts, and I couldn't talk to you at all, you know, for days. I'd be in another world. Today, I'm just tired. I'm okay. I'm alright. Let's rock n' roll.

*

I'm not a good businessman! I'm terrible! I come up with the ideas, and direct, and put the products together, but I've always needed partners to handle the money side of things. I'm too trusting, though, and Los Angeles is a crooked place. Everyone is out to fuck you, and boy, have I been fucked! I've lost hundreds of thousands of dollars, over a couple of different deals, by investing with the wrong people. They weren't – to use the Yiddish word – "kosher." I never thought that people in our business would try to destroy each other. Because that wasn't the history. That's the history of the straight business world, you know, but they came in here and did the exact same thing. You know the expression: "How do they sleep at night?" Well, how *do* they sleep at night? I have no idea. They must take pills to sleep at night, these rip-off artists and finaglers who fuck everyone over on a daily basis.

Around 2003, while I was still with Legend, I signed a five-year deal with Digital Playground. They were a brand new company, up and coming, who seemed to understand the direction of the industry. The owner was a guy named Joone. He's well-retired now, with a lot of money, living in Hawaii. But he agreed to host a Pussyman site and even bought my 15 original movies to sell online. Shortly into the deal, however, he lost interest in the sites and decided to become this big movie director instead. And he did. In the late 2000s, Digital Playground really took over. They produced some humongous hits. There was *Pirates: XXX*, a parody of *Pirates of the Caribbean*, which had a $1,000,000 budget, the largest in the history of porn. Anyway, rather than manage my site as promised, he used the page to advertise for his movies. When anyone went in search of *Pussyman*, it would just say: "Coming soon from Digital Playground."

And then, in 2004, a number of new internet distributors went into business. There was one company called Brazzers. Headquartered in Montreal. I think they're actually owned by some Eastern European corporation, but they have offices in Canada, you know, and operate a ton of websites. And there were other new companies, too, most of them from Florida. Of course, right away, I thought it was a government setup. But it was just these kids, seemingly, who had started up companies and were doing reality-based shoots for the internet. Reality Kings. The Bang Brothers. They hired beautiful women, probably dancers from South Beach. And the girls were *new*. I mean, they weren't from Los Angeles, so no one had ever seen them before. The next thing you know, these Florida companies, they put up the tube sites that broadcast other people's movies. At least, I think it was them. I don't know for sure.

Originally, you know, places would buy pictures from manufacturers to sell online. Well, manufacturers sold their movies *to brokers* who then sold them to these sites. They would carry all your movies broken down by scene. If someone happened to love this one particular actress, they could go to the site, type in her name, and – boom! – there she is. On their credit card, you know, they could buy a scene or a whole movie. Whatever. And the site got a percentage, and I got a percentage. That's how it worked. But not anymore! The movies were sold to the brokers under the assumption that these brokers wouldn't sell them to *everyone*. Well, all of a sudden, people started calling me up and saying that my movies were... everywhere! For free! Let's say, 800 movies, directed over a period of 20 years, and I hadn't copyrighted any of them. Who thought of copyright? It never crossed my mind. Seriously.

Today, on the internet, there are millions of these tube sites, all essentially run by these same companies. When you visit these sites, you only see advertisements for them. Of course, you have to pay money to browse their sites, while everyone else's stuff is available for free. And most people can watch anything to get off. They don't need anything special. But it's all there, anyway, broken down by category. If you search "small-breasted women," then you'll find a tube site of scenes with small-breasted women. If you want brunette, or legs, you know, whatever you want, you can type that in, watch a bunch of scenes, and it won't cost you any money. Like if I'm shooting a movie and want to know more about a particular actress, then I just go to the site *Freeones*. It gives me a whole breakdown. There'll be a little description of her, some information, and some pictures. And if I want to see how she performs, then I can also find a few scenes for free.

In one respect, I guess, the consumer can now see any porn they want for nothing. The people who'd been making it for years, though, and wanted to do it well, they've been basically eliminated. Most of them went out of business. And then there was the global financial crisis, and that just ruined everything completely! Even if that never happened, the porn business still would have taken a humongous tumble because of what these internet guys did. I used to collect huge royalty checks, you know, in the thousands! On the 15th of every month, checks would come pouring in from internet distributors. And now, every so often, I'll get a hundred bucks in the mail. I've gone from averaging $120,000 down to $20,000 a year. I never thought it would be like this. I mean, that's one reason why I stayed in the business for so long. I always figured, even in hard economic times, you know, porn would never fail. Boy, was I wrong!

*

At this point in my life, I could get out. Sure. Most people eventually do. And when they first leave the business, and then for some years after, they probably feel guilty. When they're my age, though, between 60 and 70, bored and retired, they think back and say, "Wow! Those were great times!" That's why a lot of these old people have groups on Facebook. Everyone's always on there, trying to get back in touch with people they knew from the '70s, you know, "The Golden Age." And they'll talk about their old movies and memories and memoirs. This and that. Da da da.

Otherwise, it's not really that hard to get out. No. You just do something else. Get a hobby. Meet new people. If a civilian person is not going to be understanding, and some won't, then that relationship will be in deep trouble. Of course, I've heard horror stories. But you hear horror stories from every entertainment field! Music and Hollywood, you know, and wrestling, more than anywhere. For the most part, in the adult world, ideal relationships work as they would for anyone. With trust and support. Okay, there are some obnoxious people who don't care about their partners and use the movies as a way to cheat. And there are others who actually *like* the fact that they're wives or girlfriends are big stars and make lots of money. They don't feel any jealousy. Me? I've had all kinds of relationships in my life. And now, at this age, if I'm really involved with someone, then that's it. I don't want any other action going on.

My last relationship was four years ago. She was an actress who made a few movies in the '90s. One day, she called, out of the blue. She wanted to be a court stenographer and needed some extra money to pay for school. So she did a couple of movies before realizing, pretty quickly, that the business had changed completely. But she liked me. And I liked her. She was smart. Had attitude. And was a heavy bodybuilder, you know, with some serious muscles. The biggest clitoris I've ever seen. She was *powerful, sexual, wild*. Courtney! That was her name! She lived in Orange County, though, so I told her: "I'm not sure if this is going to work. Orange County is like a whole other state, man, and I can't drive there." At first, she'd come here every weekend, and I went there, once or twice, by train. After a few months, I thought to myself, "Fuck it! Let's see if she wants to move in together." Maybe we could find a place in the middle, you know, like Long Beach?

She thought about it, but then got scared, and we broke up. That was my last big relationship. Since Courtney, there's only been little things. I miss it. I miss talking with a female on a regular basis, you know what I mean? Because I've been in relationships for my whole life. From the time I was 20 years old, back in New York, outside of a month or two, here and there, I've always been with someone. I'm getting old, man, and am ill so often, it would be nice to have a woman around to take care of me. But – you know something? – when someone sleeps over these days, I don't particularly like it. I'm used to being by myself, I guess. Doing what I want, when I want. I was thinking about this last week. Someone stayed over for the night, this model, a black woman, and I wanted her to leave like… right away! Whereas, in the past, you know, I would want to like *hang*.

I've always had a thing for black women, but in the last ten years, I've developed an *extra* attraction to them. Big time! I'd probably rather go out with a hot black chick than anyone. And I use them in my face-sitting movies. I told you, I'm the one who invented face-sitting. I mean, at least, I was the first person to do it in public. Out in the open. For everyone to see. Plus, I've always shot movies of black women with white guys. So now, I'm one of the few directors who do interracial face-sitting. I have tons of fans who love this, but are afraid to do it themselves. They'll write to me: "Don't you get a little nervous or embarrassed?" Why should I be embarrassed? I'm proud of what I do. And, over the years, I've gone out with some black girls, but was never seriously involved. There was Tiffany, sure, but she's only like $1/10^{th}$ black. I really do like them sexually, though, and I like them. Period.

I just haven't been seriously involved with anyone. But if I met someone who I really got along with, then I probably would, you know, because I still have a lot to offer. It's just a question of compromise. Because everyone's different, and we all carry some heavy baggage! So if you don't compromise, then the relationship is not going to work. That's the key. In any romantic relationship, you have to compromise. Well, in every relationship, really, you know, even me and my dog have to compromise.

*

I don't know. I've been in it for so long, I'm probably in it forever. Well, if the book hits, then I might do something else. Maybe teach sexuality at a college somewhere? That's always something I hoped to be doing at this age. Other than that, I don't really have many regrets. God no! I've been on a mission since the '80s to promote the power of… but I didn't. I only *half* did. If I really hustled, and stayed focused, and met the right people, you know, and didn't get ripped off in business, then I could have done *exactly* what I set out to do. And now, I'd have enough money to live on. I mean, I certainly never expected to be in this position! From being a communicator, and an educator, and an artist, to just barely making a living.

When I direct these movies, for these little amounts of money, I'm not doing what I want. Like the series I've been doing this year, *Fornication 101*. I'm supposed to be like a teacher helping the audience learn about the industry. Basically, it's a remake of those *Auditions* I did back in the '90s. They'll do a little tease, you know, and then a scene, but first, I ask them all these personal questions. *Why did you get involved in the business? Did you want to become a star? Do you like having sex in front of the camera?* I'm interested, too, because I'm old, and things have changed so much. For instance, I'll ask, "At what age did you first have sex?" Nearly everyone says 14 years old. Maybe 15, at the latest. I was shocked! It's amazing to me what goes on, not just in my business, but in the regular world, you know, with kids in high school! Anyway, when I came to this company, they looked at my old movies and decided, I guess, that these movies wouldn't cost very much to make.

This is Devil's Films. They're affiliated with a novelty company called Pipe Dreams. They used to make a line of Pussyman toys, like 30 different items, you know, and I would receive royalties every couple of months. Well, a few years ago, they bought Devil's. The owner, Nick, he was good friends with Bruce/Will Divide. So when I found out that he bought this company, I called him up and said, "Hey, Nick, let's start the *Pussyman* series again! Are you interested?" And he was. But you can't put $35-40,000 into a movie anymore. You can hardly make money putting $10,000 into a movie. So he came up with this *Fornication 101*, and that's what I'm doing. Although Nick mostly just deals with the toy company and really doesn't get too involved in the filmmaking. In fact, I hardly speak with him anymore. Originally, I thought we'd be working together, making great films, and maybe some of them would become humongous hits. But nobody cares. Get the product out. That's their attitude.

I do the best that I can, but it's pretty much impossible to make anything decent. Even for the greatest, most genius, independent filmmaker in the history of the world, you know what I mean? For instance, before Legend shut down, I made this series of cheap girl-girl orgies. Jack wanted me to take a mix of black girls, white girls, Asians, Latinas, whatever, and just shoot one long scene. He called it something like *Chocolate Latin Mocha Orgy*. I said, "That's the dumbest thing I've ever heard! Who's going to watch that for 70 straight minutes? No one." So I would just put three women in a room and shoot them for ten minutes. Do that three times, and then, at the end, put them all together for 15 minutes. Fine. There's your stupid, miserable, movie. In the old days, I came up with my own ideas, wrote my own scripts, had my own cameramen, and even hired my own editor. That's really the most important fucking thing!

Like Scorsese, for instance, he has had the same editor since the '70s. They worked on *Woodstock* together. There was just tons of film, you know, nothing was in any order. This editor, she took all that fucking footage and made *Woodstock*.

And she's been Scorsese's editor now for over 40 years. But me, when I finish a shoot now, I turn the film over to Devil's, and their editor takes over. He's not getting paid this giant salary, I'm sure, and they have him on a tight schedule. So why would he give a shit? He doesn't. That's just how it is, nowadays. How do I deal with that? I've made some movies under a different name. Sometimes, too, when I was forced to do a picture, like an anal movie, you know, or DP. That's Double Penetration. When a girls gets fucked, simultaneously, in the pussy and the ass. I hated doing those pictures, man, and I wouldn't put my name on them. So I called myself Cory Chaplin. Why? I don't know. That's just the name I used.

So it's been rather depressing for quite some time. But hey, I have a job. That's how I have to look at it. I need the money. I spent on crazy things, made some bad investments, and over the last few years, it's really come back to haunt me. I thought I'd always be making $100,000 a year. $70,000 on residuals, at least. Not that I ever cared about money. I don't need a ton of money, you know, just enough for a nice little house… and maybe a car that doesn't fucking fall apart.

*

When I was at Legend, and the budgets started going down – boom! – I should have been on the phone right away. If I contacted other companies, you know, then I would have been hired left and right. I have a tremendous résumé: hit after hit, huge series, tons of awards, the whole bit.

I'm in the Hall of Fame. *I'm in 3 Hall of Fames!* It's not like the Rock n' Roll Hall of Fame where there's a special night. No. On the same night where they give out the regular awards, you know, they bring up eight to ten people and give them a little plaque. I have mine over there with my other awards. I'll show you. This one here is from the East Coast Video Awards in the '80s. Best Comedy scene. I don't know. I couldn't act at all, and somehow, this scene won like four awards. Here's another one. When is this from? 2002. Big Bust

Specialty Picture. *That was my specialty!* But I've received numerous awards over the years. Tons of nominations. And once I became Pussyman, that clinched it for me. It was automatic. The year after the first *Pussyman* movie came out, they put me in the Hall of Fame. I'd already been in the business for so long: acting, writing, directing, and producing. And now, decades later, I'm one of a few people who've really done everything.

The AVN Hall of Fame was the biggest. For years, you know, and Paul, he's now tying to become a producer for Showtime. He has some contacts there because they broadcast the AVN Awards every year. They just made this documentary – I can't remember what it's called – that really takes you through all of the movies from the '70s. It tries to tell the story, you know, of what went on back then, and he introduces some of the legends. Because people have such short memories. And we can't tour like the legends of rock n' roll. Those music legends, they can always play shows, make a little money, and continue to do something they love. That's what I should be doing now. Going around and playing… well, I can't play guitar. But I'm a legend! In this business, though, the legends aren't respected. Yeah, once a year, they'll give them a Hall of Fame award, you know, and the rest of the year, they'll let them starve.

A few days ago, in *Billboard*, I read this tremendous interview with Eddie Van Halen, where he talked about his career, drugs and alcohol, the upcoming tour. He talked about a lot of different things. One thing he said – get this – he never listens to music. Like maybe a cut, here and there, but basically, for his whole life, he only listened to his own guitar-playing. Seriously. I couldn't believe it! I guess, it makes some sense. For the most part, I don't watch porno movies anymore. I only watch my own. And the movies made today, I usually find them rather boring. Not to my taste. Personally, I wouldn't put one on. The actors are horrible. The directors don't know what they're doing. I mean, they're *alright*, but not for big films. Not that many people even make big films anymore. So lately, no, I don't think anyone has done anything that's been really, really, really, good. Nothing stands out, you know what I mean?

I told you, the biggest picture of this century was that parody of *Pirates of the Caribbean*. Maybe *Superman vs. Batman* or *The Fast and the Furious*. I did something similar when I was at Coast to Coast, but we would change the title. Now they keep the same name and add "XXX Parody." The biggest director right now is a guy who only makes these kind of movies. Axel Braun. His father, Lasse Braun, was a famous Italian porno director from the '70s. I remember, when I first entered the industry, he had this giant hit called *Sensations* that went all over the world. Well, like ten years ago, his kid got into the business. He started small, but then made some connections, you know, and had that name, Braun, for what it's worth. And 99% of his movies are these parodies. They have huge budgets, and he wins the award every year. Pretty much everyone else just makes stupid scenes, one after another, to fill spots on their internet sites.

Most of these videos, no one ever sees. It's not like music where they can put something up on YouTube and get millions of views. Like that song from the *Furious 7* soundtrack. It just came out this year, and they've had a billion views already! It's by Wiz Khalifa, you know, with some random dopey-looking white guy. Who the fuck is this guy? I don't know. I have no idea. Whoever he is, you know, he sings the hook, and I can listen to his hook over and over and over and over.

CHAPTER 15
IT'S MY PARTY

I want to let the readers out there know, I am now a senior citizen. Yes! I've lived 65 years in these lucky United States of ours.

My birthday was yesterday, June 23rd. I'm a Cancer on the cusp of Gemini. I had my whole chart read when I was 25. For a while, in the '70s, I was *really* into it. Big time! I knew all my signs, you know, my Moon sign and my Earth sign, and I would ask everyone else about theirs. Cancers are emotional and caring. And over the years, from what I've seen, they're usually good friends with both sexes. In the porno business, there's a lot of us. More than just about any sign. The women, especially. So Cancer's my Sun sign, but my Mercury is Gemini. They're very brainy, you know, on the ball, always trying to come up with new ways of thinking. And they can talk, man, on all different subjects, but they can also be quiet. They're split between these different personalities, sometimes aggressive and sometimes passive. Every Gemini I've known has been like that. So your Mercury is really important. That's your mind sign and mine's in Gemini.

Anyway, I spent my birthday on set. I don't know why, but I like to shoot on my birthday. Yeah, birthdays and big Jewish holidays! Like Rosh Hashanah, for some reason, Jewish New Year, I love shooting then. Yesterday, they asked me to do this specialty kind of movie called *Water Works*. After I interview the girls, they do a little tease, and then... they squirt. Either by masturbating, or fucking someone, or both. It's a squirting contest, really, with four contestants. At the end of the movie, I announce the winner, and supposedly, there are tons of fans watching from home and casting their votes. Millions of them! Like the boxing announcer says, "For the thousands here ringside and the millions and millions watching around the world…" And it'll be two miserable, low-ranked, fighters, you know what I mean? *There aren't millions of people watching!* But he always says, "For the millions and millions." I love that!

What is squirting? Oh! Okay. That's when a woman has an orgasm, and then, well, ejaculates. Like a guy. There are a number of women who can do it. And many who can't. I mean, they all say that they can, but squirting can be faked. In *Pussyman 8: The Squirt Queens*, one of the best pictures of my career, the whole opening sequence is a roundtable discussion. A panel of experts debate whether or not squirting is real. Because I know some actresses who drink a lot of water beforehand and make a little cocktail. It's like a mix, you know, of water, squirt, and pee, and then, everything comes out together. Regular people can't tell the difference. *I can tell* because this is my expertise. When they squirt, it *sprays*. But when they pee water, or pee pee, it like *shoots* out! I've seen some women squirt all the way across the room. That can't be regular ejaculate! But that's what they say, and we pay them for it, and there have been a billion squirt movies made over the years.

At Coast to Coast, we actually made one of the first ones ever. I remember, at the big convention in Las Vegas, Bruce/Will Divide was cheating on his wife. You know the story: "Whatever happens in Vegas." Da da da. Well, in the morning, I went by his room to pick him up for breakfast, and the bed was totally soaked. Drenched. From squirt! At least, that's what he said. So he came up with an idea for a movie, *Rain Woman*, you know, like *Rain Man*. This was 1989, and it sold tons of copies. The star's name was Fallon, and she had orgasms like I had never seen before. When women really squirt, they have the most intense, deep, orgasms. And they can have like 50 in a row. Boom! Boom! Boom! In my squirt series for Legend, I shot this one girl, Kim Wylde. We put her on a table, and when she squirted, it hit the ceiling. She went into this frenzied, full-body orgasm. Shaking and shivering. Afterward, she just laid there, motionless, totally drained.

Until yesterday, I hadn't done one of these movies in a long time. I mean, I like doing them – of course! – I like anything to do with pussy. Plus, Cancers are very water-oriented people. Maybe that's why I like squirting, you know, water, fluid, flowing. And I'm also really into getting peed on. I told you about *House of Sin* – right? – that Avon movie where Candice pissed all over me. I loved it! The woman's above, and I'm down below, and it feels like a waterfall coming down upon me from inside of her. And it's not bad for you. I read about it. I've looked into everything, man. I've even drank female cum! I don't know if that's a thing to write down, but I don't care. Everyone in the business already knows. They know who I am.

*

My car is still in the shop, so I called Scott, and he picked me up. Scott... Johnson? To be honest, I don't know his last name. Because he changes it depending on the movie. But since I moved out here, he's been my main photographer. Not cameraman. *Photographer*. He shoots the box covers. The stills. Between scenes, you know, he takes pictures that we use for promotion. Scott also helps to set up the shoot. For a while now, he's been like my semi-production manager. On and off. And yesterday morning, he picked me up around quarter to 9:00, and we drove over to the location together.

It's only ten minutes from here. A nice, modern house that I've used many times. Huge. Two stories. In the '90s, I might have even been the first person to ever shoot there. *Pussyman 13*, I think. The owner's name is Ben and he didn't know that it was a hardcore picture. But he ended up loving the whole thing, you know, following around the performers, looking to make friends. Maybe even a few dates? Who knows? I mean, he's married. His wife's name is Paula. Grandkids and everything. And after that first shoot, they began renting their house to all these different X-rated people. They also rented the place to *Beverly Hills 90210*. Yeah, this house was on that show! For adult movies, though, they could rent it out every day, and that's basically what they've been doing for 20 years. Eventually, they bought a second house, you know, where they live now. The original house, they just rent out for film shoots.

I bet they've made millions on that place! All they have to pay for the cleaning service. The only time there's a real mess is after squirt scenes, although I told you, this is the first squirt movie I've made in forever. And it's not like you think. You're just picturing cum everywhere. I know you are! We bring towels and everything gets cleaned up. And during the shoot, the body fluids land on the woman. On her pussy, usually, you know, because I'm Pussyman. The porno producers, and the viewers, they all want it on the face. That's their favorite. The girls, most of them, they don't really care. Some of the house owners will care and cover their couches, you know, but others don't, so we just turn over the cushions. It might gross you out, I guess. That's why you don't do it! But people who don't give a shit, they can make tons of money! Like Ben. He hasn't worked a regular job in years.

Call-time was 9:00. That's when the crew, the makeup person, and the first actress are supposed to arrive. After she gets her makeup, Scott does some stills. Usually, the girl brings a bunch of her own clothes, and between me and Scott, we select an outfit. Something that will pop on the box cover, you know what I mean? While he's taking pictures, I'll talk to the real cameraman, set up the lighting, and run through our day. It was probably already 11:30 before we started shooting. And then I basically improvise the whole thing. What I say is… what I say! I mean, even in my big features, I would never go exactly word-for-word. Everything was always Larry David-style. Spontaneous! To me, especially when it comes to sex, it's much better that way. Sure, I have some friends who still do the traditional storyboards. And I will bring in a little outline in case I get lost for a second. Sometimes I share it with the performers, but for the most part, they don't care. They're only there to do a scene.

I do talk to them beforehand to find out any questions that might be off-limits. The first girl, she was very cool. Late 20s. I can't remember her name. I know, I know. It was only yesterday! There are so many models, man. So if I shoot a girl once, I only see her for a couple of hours, and then she's gone. But I liked this one a lot. She wasn't *stunning*. More like your typical girl-next-door. We had a nice talk about the business, you know, how some producers treat people like shit. And I told her about myself, and she knew it all. She must have studied porn history a little bit. So that was surprising. And she had a couple of tattoos: one on her arm and another up her side. I asked her if she planned to get more. She said, "Yeah, I want to have a kid, and when I do, I'll get one more tattoo for him. Or her. And that'll be it."

So then, of course, I interviewed her on camera. And then, after she answered my questions, I said, "Well, okay, let's see if you can squirt. All my fans are out there watching and Twittering in." When I first met with Devil's Films, I told them: "If you want me to do the same series from 20 years ago, then I have to update it. Let me throw some tweets in there! That'll be different." And I just make them up. I'll say like, "Carlos from Florida just tweeted that he wants you to squirt on his face." I don't know why, but in a previous movie, it was all Latin guys tweeting me. Scott flipped out, you know, "What are you doing, David? This is not a Latin movie!" So, yesterday, on purpose, I did a few Latin tweets. After like the third one, he went nuts! But these tweets were coming in from all over the country, man. Back east. Northwest. Someone from Denver twittered in! There were even a number from right here in Northridge, the former capital of porn.

I don't even really know much about Twitter. I've been thinking of getting on there, but I don't know how to do it. All the girls are on Twitter, and Instagram, you know, showing off! I mean, regular people are constantly showing off, so you can imagine how it is for these exhibitionists. They post pictures of themselves 24 hours a day. And it's also a way for producers to get in touch with them. So if I was on Twitter, I could contact them, and they would follow me back? Is that how it works? Okay. Maybe I'll sign up for an account, you know, and you could help me, while you're here.

*

She played with her pussy for a bit, and then I brought out the Pussyman jewelry. Did I mention the jewelry? I did? Anyway, my jewelry fit her perfectly. She put it on her giant pussy lips and squirted all over the fucking place.

And then the guy came in. Mark Wood. Very nice. Mellow. He's probably been in the business for 15 years. He's married to a porno star, too, Francesca Le', and she's also a very nice person. When she does a scene, though, she forgets about everything and goes crazy. Swallows the cock until slurp is coming down her face. I've seen her take on five guys at the same time. She's the kind of woman who just loves sex – *loves it!* – and it shows on camera. But she wasn't there. Mark Wood, her husband, he was there. In the movie, he had gone to get something at the store while I was asking my questions. When he returned, I said, "Here's your guy. I'm going to sit back and watch, you know, because that's what I do!" Their scene was tremendous. As far as quality, I would rate it very high. At the end, she said, "How was that? Did I win the contest?" And I said, "You did great. When the votes come in, I'll let you know."

The second girl, Missy Monroe, I remember from years ago, when she was much younger. Missy wasn't my type, really. She was just a wild, filthy, performer. And the company, they told me that she could still squirt, so they hired her. She drove all the way here from Las Vegas, and probably stayed in Los Angeles for the night, hoping to get another scene while she's in town. When she came in, she didn't look the same. I hardly recognized her. I said, "Hey, Missy. Long time, no see. Are you still as wild you used to be?" I asked her a few questions, but she didn't seem to be very interested. I mean, it was difficult to have a conversation. Once she grabbed one of those Pipe Dreams dildos, however, the next thing you know, she was fucking squirting everywhere.

I yelled for my assistant. I could have just called him in, but for some reason, I decided to *scream*. He was played by an actor named Will Power. I've used him before, and he's alright. I like him, you know, but on a baseball team, he'd be the utility man. He does the job, you know what I mean? And when he opened the door, Missy said, "Oh, you look hot." Or something like that. I don't know. It just came out of her mouth. And then, you know, they went through the positions. She gave him head. They fucked. She squirted. I said, "Don't forget, man. You have to give her head, too." So he threw her legs back, and the cameraman went in for a close-up. And she was pulling on her lips because they were so big. I was shocked! Both of these girls had giant pussy lips. I don't see that very much anymore. I used to see it a lot, especially when I did my series *Pussyman's Giant Pussy Lips*, you know, when I was at Legend and had those different lines.

After Will Power did the old "pop shot," you know, that basically ended my day. No one knew it was my birthday. What were they going to do? Buy me a cake? Throw it on top of my head? Like these days, in baseball, how they throw pies in each other's faces after the game. Yeah, every time someone knocks in the game-winning run, even if it's a little bloop single, here comes a pie in the face! It's horrible! Max Scherzer, he just pitched a no-hitter for the Nationals last week, and his teammates ran out and squirted him with chocolate syrup. He had fudge all over his face, dripping onto his shirt. It looked like he was covered in liquid shit! Who wants that after pitching a no-hitter? I don't think anyone wants that. I would *hate* it. I'm not really into food on my body. I guess, there are some people who like food, you know, that turns them on.

I remember shooting a scene at the house of one of my former cameramen who loved kitchen sex. This guy was my leading cameraman for a while, you know, until 9/11, when he became one of those people who would constantly battle me on the set. But this scene was back in the '90s. I had the actor, Dave Hardman, go into the kitchen and bring out some food. He was a well-known porno star for years, and when it came to sex, he was up for anything! In this scene, he dumped cereal on top of his head. And then put a doughnut on his cock while the woman gave him a blowjob. He was loving it, you know, dumping more and more cereal on himself. And my cameraman was so happy! I must have done some other food scenes over the years, because I've made so many fucking movies. They don't do anything for me. It's all just so disgusting. Food mixed together with sweat and cum.

Now there you go. *That's a real mess!*

*

After a long shoot, man, as soon as I get home, I'll pass out. Immediately. That's what happens. Yesterday, I got back at 5:30, fed the dog, and all of a sudden, it was pitch dark. Middle of the night. And then, of course, you know, I was awake for hours and never went back to sleep. It's affected me all day. My eyes are half-closed over here. And my back is killing me!

I have to shoot the rest of the movie tomorrow. Two more scenes. The top two stars. There's a little blonde girl, Loni Evans. I've shot her once before, and she was very cordial, you know, didn't cause any trouble. That's something you look for, nowadays, because some of these stars will cause trouble. Just for the hell of it! They'll complain for an hour, take their money, and leave. This and that. They might bring in their boyfriend or someone from outside of the industry, and that can be a complete failure. Other times, they just refuse to work and throw a fit. A *hissy fit*, you know what I mean? Walk off of the set. The other girl tomorrow is Sarah Van… I don't know. Sarah Van Something or Other. She's a name, you know, a big star. We'll see. Scott said that he's worked with her many times, and they get along great. She calls him a friend.

When it's finished, I'll drop off the footage with Devil's. And then I'll see it… when it comes out. They give me a few copies, you know, but who cares. I used to care! At Snatch, we could take as many Pussyman tapes as we wanted. I kept boxes in the trunk of my car, and for a while there, I didn't have to pay for very much. At the gas stations, they had those little stands where they sell magazines and videos, you know, DVDs. I would give them three or four DVDs, and they would fill up my tank. Oh yeah. I traded DVDs in exchange for food, clothes, *anything*. I remember, one time, I was living with Sana Fey on the border of Mar Vista and Santa Monica. We had a guy over to hook up the internet. Near the computer, there were these huge bookcases lined with hundreds of porno movies. I said, "Do you want some?" And he got real nasty with me: "What do you think, I like that kind of stuff?" I was like, "Calm down, man. I'm not forcing it on you." I was just being nice!

The tapes don't mean much anymore. They still sell them, of course, Devil's Films, but there's not many bookstores left. There's not that many distributors even left to sell to the bookstores! Devil's will still sell some to foreign cable, and regular cable, and a few internet companies. And you can buy them directly on their site. But I don't give a shit. I already got paid. I used to make $3,000-5,000 for a movie, you know, plus "backends"! The director gets between 10-20% of the budget. So for this stupid $10,000 movie, I made a lousy, fucking $1200. That's what it's down to. Originally, I was supposed to do a movie for Devil's every two months, but lately, it's been every three or four months. They'll let me know like a month in advance. Or I'll call them, you know, if there's nothing on the schedule. It just depends on what game those assholes are playing. Like right now, I have no idea when I shoot for them next.

I do have a face-sitting shoot coming up. I make those for Glenn on his site *MeanBitches*. He puts different kinds of "femdom" things up there: foot worship, ass worship, face-sitting. Glenn does tons of other stuff, too. He's on Twitter every second! And he has a podcast on his own radio network. The King Adult Broadcast Network. That's him, Glenn King, and he's been getting more and more traffic. His show is called "ManEaters." It's also on TV, every Friday night, on – what's it called? – Roku. He just made a deal with them. "ManEaters" is like *The Tonight Show*. I feel I'm watching Jimmy Fallon, you know, with all his little games. Except Glenn makes them sexual. He'll have like "eating apples off girls' asses." That kind of shit. He came up with these ideas, you know, when he saw where the business was going. A number of these stations have been popping up on the internet lately where porno people have their own shows.

I met Glenn like ten years ago. He came from the computer business, and he loved face-sitting. So when I met Glenn, he had seen my *Pussy Power* movies, you know, the ones that I made for Big Top. He was a big fan! And he was this internet wiz, so I said, "Hey, I only have regular porno sites. How about making a fetish site for me?" And now, he's my neighbor! I told you, when I visited him, I saw the FOR SALE sign, and the tremendous dog park was up the street. He used to have a nice dog who I sometimes would take care of. His new dog isn't so nice. This fucking dog actually bit me right near my balls! So I don't go into his house anymore. I can't. I won't. The dog knows he got me. The last time that I was there, he just stared at me, you know, like I was prey.

But Glenn is tremendous and has really helped me out. And he's honest, you know, something rare in this business. My site on *MeanBitches* is called "Deviant David." Glenn came up with the name. I didn't want to use Pussyman. These aren't like big movies or anything, just little scenes, and I'm not really the director. I'm in them, you know, getting face-sat. That's my thing. I'm the greatest to ever do it! The girl will squash me, so I can't breathe. Although, now, I also will have her talk to the fans while she's sitting on me. She'll say, "Look at this pathetic guy! He's been in the porno business for 40 years. And now, he can't fuck anymore, so he just gets face-sat. Do you losers want to end up like this?" It's a goof, you know, and it's tremendous! And my fans, the people who've been watching me forever, they know it's me. David Christopher. Yeah, my hair is whiter, but other than that, I look the same. I haven't changed.

*

Jack called me yesterday, you know, from Legend. Out of the blue. I hadn't spoken to him in two years. He wanted to wish me a happy birthday. And then I got like 40 birthday wishes on Facebook, at least. Mostly from people that I never correspond with, you know what I mean? Some of them, I don't even know. Who are these people? I have no idea.

When I first got on Facebook, I didn't have any trouble, but then I hit something by accident and ended up posting this nasty picture: a big ass sitting on my face. A fan must have sent it to me, but I didn't know how to delete it! And you know on the bottom, where the messages pop up? Well, it never says how to reply. So I'll write like five lines back to somebody and then I'm stuck. I can't send back an instant message! This is easy stuff, you know, for any regular person, except for those of us who grew up in a different era. Some of it is obnoxious, though, too, like how people will lie and put up pictures of themselves from 20 years ago. Not me, man. My picture was taken right here in the backyard, one afternoon when I first moved in. I look like a cool rock n' roller. Sunglasses. A joint in my mouth. And I'm with my dogs, you know, Trinity's up front, and Lola, she's lying on the ground.

She didn't make it to the dog park yesterday. None of my dog park friends could take her, unfortunately. I have this one friend, John, who helps a lot with Lola, and another friend, Marley. Well, the dog's name is Marley. I don't know many of the owner's names. Except for a bunch of guys named Richard. I met them all at once: Richard, Rick, Richie. No Dicks. Nobody calls themself Dick anymore. Because of the word, of course, but I think it's also because of Dick Cheney. No one wants to be Dick after him! One of these Richards is a photographer and – get this – he shot John Lennon on the day he was killed. He was Annie Leibovitz' assistant, and they were taking pictures for *Rolling Stone*. Only a couple of hours later, they heard the news. After that, for 25 years, he worked for in Asia, you know, Cambodia and Laos. He now works for the Associated Press in their Los Angeles office. I bet he has some stories, man. Enough for a book like this.

I have to say, this has been very interesting for me. I've enjoyed it, you know, the opportunity to tell my stories and rehash the early times with my parents and Bonnie, and in New York, and through the years. I mean, I have the memories in my head, but I don't get a chance to talk about them very often. I'm glad you're getting them now before I really start to forget! Because what I've been talking about, basically, it's my history. And one of the reasons why I've always liked history, you know, is that you get to see how it all went down, how we got here, where we are, today. A lot of it is just fate. Destiny. I remember, in college, walking around New York, seeing the first bookstores, and thinking to myself, "If I don't make it as a teacher, and my father doesn't force me to take over State Beef, then maybe I could do something with this." And then – boom! – I was on a fucking porno set. I went from the meat business to the meat business! That's what my friends always say.

Okay. Are we finished? By this point, I've said a whole shitload. I don't know. I've just been talking and talking. But I don't think I've missed too many things. I've explained all my philosophies, right? Why I did this and why I did that. I told you about how I drove around Sharon wearing women's panties! I told you that I worship Amazon goddesses, to this day, because of my 5th grade teacher. And I how I turned my wife/girlfriend into a famous dominatrix. And how, in the '90s, I became this humongous personality, Pussyman, and that's when I was really at my best, you know, creatively. I must have broken every rule in the business. Although, really, those were just movies about me, being myself, running a company, and searching for women with... great pussies! Who were *empowered* in their sexuality. And I wanted to show how that was a good thing. I still try to do that. I'm still plugging along. I've never quit.

Even though, I told you, how my movies were stolen and put on the internet for free. And even though I've had these sore throats forever and am sick all the fucking time! No. My work isn't over. Not at all. I still hope, somehow, in the modern way, to keep communicating my beliefs about the power of female sexuality. Which was repressed for years and years and years. But I've said that already. I know. What else can I say?

I went and saw the new Mad Max movie. *Fury Road*. It was tremendous. Nonstop action. Incredible camerawork. Spectacular landscapes. That opening sequence, where the water comes falling out of the mountain. Brilliant! I really have to give the director his credit. George Miller. He only does these Mad Max movies, and he hadn't made one in 30 fucking years! He must be my age, you know, the first Mad Max was made in the '70s, and then *Road Warrior* and *Thunderdome*.

It was about the long road. Through the desert. It reminded me of Los Angeles, you know, because we're in the middle of this horrible drought. And just like the bad guy in the movie, we have CEOs doing their best to keep all our water for themselves. They have gallons of it stashed away somewhere. Without a doubt. These patriarchal corporations and military guys, in some way or another, they've ruined everything. I mean, the whole world is dying. As the climate changes, you know what I mean? I also read somewhere that George Miller was trying to make *Mad Max* into this whole women's movie. And he did. It's called *Mad Max*, yeah, but Charlize Theron is the main character. Max is just like her sidekick. And these hot wives, they were sick of being that warmonger's sex slaves. Charlize Theron lead them away. She wanted to take them to some "green place" where there was water and gardens and everything. Paradise!

When they got there, they found these old women, the matriarchs, but most of them had died, and the "green place" had been destroyed. So Charlize Theron, Max, the hot wives, and these old ladies, they all jumped in the truck together and headed back down the road. To go kick some ass! This really was a female power movie, you know what I mean? I was very impressed. I give it huge ratings. *Fury Road*. It was a masterpiece! And at the end, you know, he had that tremendous quote. I don't remember it exactly, but it was something like... wait. Let's search for it. Google "Quote... at the end of..." *Mad Max*. There it is, man. It comes right up! What does it say? "Where must we go, we who wander this wasteland, in search of our better selves?" Wow! George Miller! For a Hollywood action picture, this guy is trying to make a statement! Big time!

"Where must we go, we who wander this wasteland, in search of our better selves?" Good fucking question!

SOUNDTRACK

"Dream Lover" – Bobby Darin (1959)
"96 Tears" – ? (Question Mark) and the Mysterians (1966)
"In-a-Gadda-da-Vida" – Iron Butterfly (1968)
"Volunteers" – Jefferson Airplane (1969)
"Baba O'Riley" – The Who (1971)
"Gloria" – Patti Smith (1975)
"More, More, More" – Andrea True Connection (1976)
"Sweet Dreams" – Eurythmics (1983)
"Real American" – Rick Derringer (1985)
"Like a Prayer" – Madonna (1989)
"California Love" – 2Pac ft. Dr. Dre (1996)
"American Idiot" – Green Day (2000)
"Who Knew" – P!nk (2006)
"American Oxygen" – Rihanna (2015)
"See You Again" – Wiz Khalifa ft. Charlie Puth (2015)

&

"Lola" – The Kinks (1970) R.I.P.

For Abe and Frances
and Bonnie

Publisher's Note

The contents of this book are Bernie Cohen a.k.a. David Christopher's personal memoirs of how he experienced and interpreted the events detailed in this book. They are in no way meant to be a historical accounting. The thoughts, opinions and recollections in no way reflect the opinions of Matthew Klane or the publisher. This book is intended purely for entertainment purposes.

About the Author

Matthew Klane is a writer, artist, and professor living in Albany, NY. He is Bernie Cohen's nephew.